Dr Karl's Collection of Great Australian Facts & Firsts

Dr Karl Kruszelnicki

Angus&Robertson
An imprint of HarperCollins*Publishers*

Angus&Robertson
An imprint of HarperCollins*Publishers*, Australia

Ears, Gears and Gadgets, Forests, Fleece and Prickly Pears and *Flight, Food and Thingummyjigs*
first published as *Science and Technology* and *People and Achievements* by HBJ Group, Australia,
1988; revised in 1997 and published by HarperCollins*Publishers* (under the Angus&Robertson
imprint) as Books 1, 2 and 3 of the series *Great Australian Facts and Firsts*.

This combined edition first published in Australia in 2002
Reprinted in 2002
by HarperCollins*Publishers* Pty Limited
ABN 36 009 913 517
A member of the HarperCollins*Publishers* (Australia) Pty Limited Group
www.harpercollins.com.au

Text copyright © Karl Kruszelnicki Pty Ltd 1997
Illustrations copyright © Gus Gordon 1997

HarperCollins*Publishers*
25 Ryde Road, Pymble, Sydney, NSW 2073, Australia
31 View Road, Glenfield, Auckland 10, New Zealand
77–85 Fulham Palace Road, London W6 8JB, United Kingdom
Hazelton Lanes, 55 Avenue Road, Suite 2900, Toronto, Ontario M5R 3L2
and 1995 Markham Road, Scarborough, Ontario M1B 5M8, Canada
10 East 53rd Street, New York NY 10032, USA

National Library of Australia Cataloguing-in-Publication data:

Kruszelnicki, Karl, 1948– .
Dr Karl's collection of great Australian facts & firsts.
Includes index.
For primary school students.
ISBN 0 207 19860 8.
1. Natural history – Australia – Juvenile literature. 2. Science – Australia – Juvenile literature.
3. Technology – Australia – Juvenile literature. 4. Inventions – Australia – Juvenile literature.
5. Australia – Social life and customs – Juvenile literature. 6. Australia – Biography – Juvenile
literature. I. Title. II. Title: Great Australian facts and firsts.
500

Front cover photograph by Karin Catt
Cover design by Christa Edmonds, HarperCollins Design Studio
Printed and bound in Australia by Griffin Press on 80gsm Econoprint

8 7 6 5 4 3 2   02 03 04 05

Thanks

This book is a compilation of three books that were originally released in 1988. In 1997, I did a major and extensive edit for re-release, so the text was very different. This 2002 release has two new features. First, it has all three previous books collected into one single volume. Second, we have fixed up any mistakes that we could find — especially the box on how 525 square metres of wing can keep a 400-tonne jumbo 747 flying. However, this book is a compilation rather than a complete rewrite, so some pieces of information are almost certainly out of date and a few mistakes may have snuck through into this edition.

As usual, there's a swag of people involved in a project such as this, and I love to thank them for all their help.

Firstly, I would like to thank the fabulous Caroline Pegram, who can find any information in the known Universe in less than 30 seconds. Secondly, once again I'd like to thank Karin Catt (we love you) for coming up with another wonderful photograph for the front cover.

Thirdly, I thank the people at HarperCollins who designed the book and got it happening and who edited it: James Herd, Christa Edmonds, Lisa Berryman, Emma Kelso and Rod Stuart, who never let his tight leopard-skin pants get in the way of his proofreading skills. Thanks also to Alison Urquhart and Shona Martyn.

Finally, I would like to offer a free service to our readers.

We have set up a special homepage where you, the reader, can post your question (in the Self Service Science section of our homepage), and where teams of scientists from around the world will attempt to help you. The URL is www.abc.net.au/science/k2. It currently has over four million words on it, and in the last week of November 2001 we had 452,059 page impressions or hits.

Two small pieces of advice: first, don't wait until the last minute and then try to get somebody else to do your homework for you. Second, it is probably worthwhile to begin your question with: *Hi, I'm a student at a primary school/secondary school/university/etc, and my question is* ... This means that the regulars on the Self Service Science forum will not say, 'Hey, we did that 10 months ago', and instead will look kindly upon your question.

Contents

Ears, Gears & Gadgets

Contents

Escape from Gallipoli

Australian soldiers have always been inventive. At Gallipoli they even invented a rifle that fired by itself, but probably never killed anybody. Instead, their invention saved thousands of lives!

The First World War began in 1914 and Turkey soon aligned itself with Germany. The Allied Forces decided to attack Turkey. In November 1914, the very first convoy of Anzacs (ANZAC stands for Australian and New Zealand Army Corps) left for the Middle East. They landed on a beach on the Gallipoli Peninsula in Turkey on 25 April 1915.

It was the wrong beach. In the dark before dawn, their landing craft had accidentally drifted past the chosen beach, thanks to the strong currents. It was just after dawn when they went ashore in a little bay that was later called Anzac Cove.

Anzac Cove has a very narrow beach, with a 100-metre-high hill behind it. Sixteen thousand Anzacs had landed by the end of that first day, but the Turks had had advance warning of their arrival. The Turks didn't want to be invaded, so they threw their forces against the invaders. By the end of that first Anzac day, the Anzacs had already suffered 2000 casualties. But by taking advantage of little hills and valleys, they were able to start digging trenches. Once they were in a trench, they were safe from the bullets, and could keep on digging.

The campaign soon turned into a stalemate. The Anzac forces couldn't advance because the Turks had the advantage of fighting on their home territory, as well as the advantage of a superior position. But the Turks couldn't throw the Anzacs off Turkish soil, because they had built their trenches too well.

Both sides had dug themselves into trenches, which were sometimes as close as 5 metres apart! The furthest the Anzacs managed to advance during the whole Anzac campaign was a single kilometre inland.

As the months rolled by into the northern hemisphere summer, around June and July, the heat increased and the conditions for the Anzacs trapped on the tiny beach became worse. Disease broke out among the troops, thanks to the flies and the very small amounts of water that the troops were allowed to have. A plague of body lice made everybody extremely miserable. And, of course, the shooting

The Periscope Rifle

In some parts of Gallipoli, the Turkish and Australian trenches were as close as five metres apart. The rifle fire was virtually continuous, so any soldier who looked over the top of his trench would have his head blown off. Lance-Corporal Beech, of Sydney, rigged up a device that let him shoot without looking over the top of the trench. He invented the Periscope Rifle. A periscope is a box with two mirrors in it, one at the top and one at the bottom. If you look in through the mirror at the bottom, you can see out through the mirror at the top. Beech had rigged up a makeshift periscope and tied it onto his rifle with some pieces of wire. The top mirror was lined up so that it looked along the rifle sights. This meant that he could poke the rifle over the top of the trench and aim it, without making himself a target.

On 19 May 1915, Major Thomas Blamey, later to become Field Marshall Blamey, saw men fiddling with bits of wood, wire and mirrors attached to a rifle. He asked them what they were building. They told him that it was an arrangement 'you can hit with, without being hit.'

Blamey got the Army to set up a small factory on the beach to make more of these periscope rifles. Even though the periscope rifles were made with bits of scrap, they were still a deadly accurate weapon up to 300 metres.

continued, and soldiers on both sides were killed or wounded. Then winter began. The tired and exhausted Anzacs were hit by an icy blizzard. Many soldiers suffered from frostbite, while others actually froze to death.

The Anzacs couldn't advance (because of the strong Turkish defence) and they couldn't stay (because of the weather). The only option was to retreat.

Unfortunately, a retreat would mean incredibly high casualties among the Anzacs. If the Turks realised that the Anzacs were leaving their trenches, they would then charge to the top of the cliffs and start firing down onto the beach in Anzac Cove. The Anzacs would be sitting ducks.

General Hamilton, the overall commander in the region, advised the British Government that in the event of a retreat from Gallipoli they could expect casualties of 50%. This caused a great upset back at Allied Headquarters in London. General Hamilton was fired, Cabinet Ministers resigned and the Secretary of State for War, Lord Kitchener himself, went to the region, the Dardanelles, to assess the situation.

Nevertheless, on 8 December 1915, the order to withdraw was issued. The Australian Prime Minister, Billy Hughes, was advised by a secret message from the British War Office that up to 50% of the Australian troops could die during the retreat.

Some 40,000 Anzacs had to be withdrawn by 19 December. The retreat began immediately. Twenty thousand Anzacs were taken out gradually, at night. The remaining Anzacs did everything to make the Turks think that nothing had changed. Even though there were fewer soldiers, the same number of fires were lit each night. The mules were led from here to there and back again, soldiers were kept on the move and the digging of trenches continued at the usual rate.

The Good Die Young

In the wars of Napoleon, only the strongest, tallest and fittest of young Frenchmen went to fight. So many of these young soldiers were killed that, by the end of the Napoleonic Wars, the average height of a Frenchman had been reduced by 15 cm.

The plan was to evacuate the next 10,000 Anzacs on the night of 18 December and the final 10,000 the night after that. But how could they avoid the tremendous casualties that would occur once the Turks realised that they were retreating?

Bill Scurry, a 20-year-old architectural model maker, and a soldier in the Seventh Battalion, knew how great a problem this was. He wrote: *It seemed impossible that we could sneak away from under Abdul's nose without a cost in casualties as great as the landing.* Bill Scurry thought that if he could design a rifle that would keep on firing during the evacuation on 19 December, the Turks would think that the Anzacs were still in their trenches.

His first device was based on the hourglass — a glass bottle through which sand trickles slowly from one compartment to another. It didn't work. First of all, the sand would stick to the glass and not flow evenly. Second, when it did flow, it applied a gradually increasing force on the trigger of the rifle, not a sudden pull.

His next idea was better — it had a delicately balanced weight attached to the rifle's trigger. Water flowed from one container to another, and eventually the second container overbalanced, which pushed the weight over and pulled the trigger. It worked every time!

mon p'tit choux! *

BEFORE   AFTER

*'my little cabbage'
('you shrimp!')

11

Bill and an 18-year-old fellow soldier and ex-school friend, A.H. 'Bunty' Lawrence, started work making as many of these self-firing rifles as they could. They needed many rifles to fool the Turkish soldiers, because each rifle would fire only once.

Once the sun had gone down on 18 December, 10,200 Anzacs were quietly taken off the beach and out to waiting ships at sea.

The day of the final withdrawal, 19 December, was a very long day for the remaining Anzacs. They even played a game of cricket, to keep up appearances. If the Turks were to suddenly attack, they would easily win, but that day the Turks just let off the usual random rifle and machine-gun rounds, as well as the occasional bomb.

The 10,000 remaining Anzacs had been broken up into three groups, A, B, and C. The A group began leaving as soon as it was dark, followed by the B group, and then the C group.

Sir John Monash was the head of an infantry brigade at Gallipoli. He wrote: *Down dozens of little gullies leading down from the front-lines came little groups of six to a dozen men, the last (in every case an officer) closing the gully with a previously prepared frame of barbed wire ... all these little columns of men kept joining up like so many rivulets which flow into the main stream, and so at last they coalesced into four continuous lines ... without check each line marched (like so many ghostly figures in the dim light) in single file to the allotted jetty.*

Once it was time for the C group to leave, they began to activate the self-firing rifles. The last soldiers in C group, just 106 men, began to move out around two a.m. To cover their departure, a dozen soldiers, including Scurry and Lawrence, stayed behind for another 45 minutes. They were as close as 20 metres to the Turks in their trenches, and they had to move around quietly, setting up more self-firing rifles.

Once the last batch of rifles had been set up, these last 12 Anzacs quietly moved down the beach.

Watch Made the New Turkey

Turkey in 1915 was a fairly powerful country, but was in danger of being taken over by other countries. The same group of people had been running Turkey for centuries. The Turkish language used an alphabet different from other western countries so the people rarely read about what was happening elsewhere. Most of the people could not read anyway, and also, the general health of the Turkish population was very low.

Kemal Atatürk was the person who changed all of this. Even though he died in 1938, he is still honoured in Turkey.

He was actually given the name Mustafa when he was born in 1881. But at secondary school, he was given the nickname Kemal, which means 'The Perfect One', because he was so good at mathematics. In 1934, after his great victories, the General National Assembly of Turkey gave him the name Atatürk, which means 'Father of the Turks'.

As a military officer he was in charge of the defence of Gallipoli when the Allied Forces tried to invade Turkey. During a major battle, he was hit in the chest by a piece of shrapnel, which should have killed him. Luckily, it hit a watch that he carried in his shirt pocket! As a result of his great success at Gallipoli, he was given the title 'Saviour of Istanbul', and was promoted to Colonel on 1 June 1915.

Like all the retreating Anzacs before them, they had wrapped their boots in layers of torn blankets to muffle the sound. They had also covered the blades of their bayonets with cloth, to stop them glinting in the moonlight.

Just as they were about to board the boats that would take them to safety, their own troops set off three powerful mines near the Turks. Monash goes on to write that: *a tornado of rifle and machine gun fire burst forth ... showing that the Turks, far from suspecting our real manoeuvre, had actually been expecting an attack. ... Thus, dramatically, with the bullets whistling harmlessly overhead, we drew off in the light of the full moon, mercifully screened by a thin mist — and so ended the story of the Anzacs on Gallipoli ... It was a brilliant conception, brilliantly organised and brilliantly executed.*

Others were amazed that it had worked so well. 'Pompey' Elliot wrote: *Looking back now, I still cannot understand how, unless their eyes were blinded, we could have eluded their vigilance, for in many places, the trenches were only metres apart.*

Not one life was lost in the evacuation, and there were only two injuries. The Anzacs' most brilliant victory was their retreat.

In the Anzac campaign at least 33,000 men died, 8587 of them Australians. Altogether, in World War I, 418,809 Australians volunteered. Of these 60,284 were killed and 152,171 were wounded.

More than 4% of the population of Australia at that time was killed or wounded in the war. It is very difficult for any nation to recover from such huge losses.

On a percentage basis, Australia suffered heavier losses of human life than any other country in the British Empire. Of the soldiers who were actually on the front line, Australia had the most casualties, at 68%, while South Africa had the least, at 8%.

The Better Machine Gun

Another 'rough-and-ready' mechanic was Corporal A.R. Muirhead, who served in France in World War I.

Lewis Light Machine Guns had bullets in little drums that were reusable and Corporal Muirhead worked out a new and better way to reload these drums with bullets. When he had leave, he took his model to present to the Army Office. But he was out of luck — somebody else had already come up with the same idea!

Still, the Army Office had another big problem for him to solve: heavy machine-guns were constantly jamming. Both sides thought that it was important to have faster ways of killing soldiers, but neither side had worked out a way to stop machine guns from jamming.

In most machine guns, the bullets were stored in a belt, not in a drum or a magazine. The belt was fed into the gun on one side. The bullets were fed from the belt into the machine-gun barrel and were then fired. The empty belt came out of the machine gun on the other side. Then it was loaded with more bullets to be used again.

Corporal Muirhead worked all night on the problem. The very next morning he had a working model of an improved belt. It was made out of a picture hook, some clothes pegs and fencing wire.

A production prototype was built within a fortnight, but by then Muirhead had had another brainwave. Machine-gun belts were always being dropped on the ground and being damaged. There had to be a better way. His brainwave was to have disposable machine-gun belts. And he was very revolutionary in saying that the belts were to be made of paper! But he was right. Within six weeks thousands of machine-gun belts made of paper came pouring off the production lines.

In World War I, all the Australian soldiers were volunteers. They were the most generous people of their generation. Geoffrey Blainey wrote, in his *A Shorter History of Australia,* that the *most drastic effect of the war upon Australia ... was the loss of all those talented people who would become prime ministers and premiers, judges, divines, engineers, teachers, doctors, poets, inventors and farmers, the mayors of towns and the leaders of trade unions, and the fathers of another generation of Australians.*

Diggers

General Ian Hamilton sent a famous message to the Australian troops, immediately after they had landed: 'Dig, dig, dig.' And that's why Aussie soldiers call themselves 'diggers'.

Rainmaking

People have always wanted to change the weather, if only a little bit. They made sacrifices to rain gods, they used magic and they danced special rain dances. The Hopi Indians of northeastern Arizona would hold a nine-day rite, usually in August. On the ninth day the dancers would carry live snakes in their mouths. Finally the snakes would be released. Wherever the snakes went, they would carry the requests of the Hopi Indians for rain.

Others tried different methods. In the early days of the Vietnam War, the American military dumped a chemical they called 'Olive Oil' on the Ho Chi Minh Trail, with the idea of forcing clouds to dump rain over the trail — making it much muddier and harder for the enemy to move supplies. Project Popeye was unsuccessful. However, there are many in the American military who think that experiments with weather control should continue to be funded.

Australian scientists were among the first to make rain. About 80% of Australia is really quite hard to live in, because it's so dry. It is the driest inhabited continent on earth. The average annual rainfall in Australia is 420 mm.

Thirty per cent of Australia is very, very dry. It gets even less than 200 mm of rain per year. This is much, much less than the world average of 660 mm. So Australians have always been ready to listen to ideas about how to make rain. Professor Pepper was the first non-Aboriginal Australian to try rainmaking, back in 1882. He used rockets to explode dynamite into the clouds. To his surprise, this didn't work. His next plan was to fly a kite up into the clouds. He thought the kite could jiggle around and excite the clouds so much that they would release rain. But he couldn't even get the kite to fly! He 'packed up and went home' and never tried making rain again.

There was a very long, and very severe, drought in 1902. It prompted another group of people to try and make rain. Clement Wragge was the group leader. (Wragge was the first person to give names to cyclones, because he thought this would make people more interested in the weather. Wragge's biggest problem was his temper. It was so bad that his nickname was 'Inclement' Wragge!) He tried to make rain at Charleville, Queensland, where he exploded two rockets into the sky. But only a few drops of rain fell — not even enough to wet the huge crowd watching him, let alone break the drought!

Clouds

Clouds are made by water vapour condensing into either tiny water droplets or ice particles. These are between 5 and 75 microns across (a human hair is about 70 microns across). These particles are so light that even gentle wind currents can hold them up.

There are four main types of clouds. They are usually classified by their height above the ground.

High clouds are usually at levels of 8 km or more above sea level. These clouds contain ice particles.

Middle clouds are made from water droplets, and are usually about 3 to 6 km above the ground.

Low clouds are also made from water droplets, and are usually less than 1.5 km above the ground. The thick and dark low clouds often give rain or snow.

Clouds with verticle development can reach from less than 1.5 km to over 13 km above the ground. Some of the heavy and dark clouds in this group can give sudden showers.

None of the people who were studying rainmaking really knew what they were doing. They needed science. The science behind rainmaking happened by accident in a deep-freeze box in the General Electric Research Laboratories in Schenectady in New York State. Two scientists, Irving Langmuir and Vincent Schaefer, were experimenting with a small cold-box with an artificial cloud in it. They discovered that when they dropped tiny particles of dry ice (frozen carbon dioxide) through the cloud, the floating water droplets in the cloud turned into ice pellets, which then began to fall.

Names of Cyclones – Wragge

Clement Wragge, who started the trend of naming cyclones, would sometimes name especially nasty and major storms after politicians who would not support his ideas. This had two benefits. First, the general public became more aware of his activities – he would become a 'public figure'. Second, the public would link devastating storms with the government, and especially the party the target politician was a member of!

Immediately, several groups around the world, including the Division of Cloud Physics of the CSIR (Council for Scientific and Industrial Research from 1926 to 1949, when it became the CSIRO) in Australia, tried to use this scientific information to make rain. They knew that clouds have water drops that are so tiny they just float. They thought that if they could turn tiny, floating water droplets in real clouds into falling ice pellets, the ice would melt back into water on the way down to the ground.

They soon found that only some clouds make rain. The rain wouldn't happen if the cloud had only water vapour in it. The clouds needed water vapour as well as tiny particles of some sort. The particle acts like a seed to start things moving, so they called the whole process 'cloud seeding'. From a tiny seed, a raindrop can grow into something big enough to fall down to the ground. In nature, ice pellets, bacteria or dust particles (maybe even from comets, like Halley's Comet or Hale-Bopp) can act as a seed or a nucleus.

First, the scientists tried dry ice. They soon found that other small particles, such as silver iodide, would also set off this process of expanding the raindrops. The silver iodide crystal is a 'good' seed — not only is it cheaper and lighter than dry ice, it even has a shape similar to a natural ice particle.

Only certain clouds can be seeded. The right type of cloud is really cold at its top — in fact, colder than 8°C below freezing point. These clouds must have more than 0.1 gram of liquid water, and should have less than 10,000 ice particles, in each cubic metre.

Water droplets that come in contact with the seed turn into ice crystals. The ice crystals then fall through the cloud, growing bigger and bigger as more water droplets stick onto them. They grow to form large snowflakes. As the snowflakes fall, they meet warmer air coming off the ground. The snowflakes melt and turn into raindrops, which wet the dry soil.

Rain — Little and Lots

One of the driest parts of the whole world is the Desierto de Atacama, in Chile. A few times each century, small parts of this desert may get some rain, but most of it gets no rain at all.

The heaviest 24-hour rainfall ever recorded happened at Cilaos, on the island of La Réunion, which is in the Indian Ocean. On 15 and 16 March 1952, a rainfall of 187 cm fell in one 24-hour period. This works out to 3424 tonnes of rain falling onto each hectare!

The heaviest rain over a calendar month was recorded in Cherrapunji, in Meghalaya, in northeastern India. In this region, air from the Bay of Bengal, loaded with moisture, has to rise over the Khasi Hills. In July 1861, 9.3 metres of rain were recorded.

This location also holds the world record for the greatest rainfall over a 12-month period. Between 1 August 1860 and 31 July 1861, 26.46 metres of rain fell.

CSIR had their first big rainmaking success on 5 February 1947. They dumped 70 kg of dry ice from a DC-3 into a cloud west of Lithgow, New South Wales. The cloud went wild. It exploded into a giant mushroom, and rain poured down within minutes. More than 12 mm of rain fell over an area of 80 square kilometres. The rain lasted for a few hours. The cloud seeded with the dry ice was the only one in the area to drop rain.

This was the first time ever recorded that humans had actually caused a decent rainstorm, and that the rain had made it all the way down to the ground. (There had been an earlier case. American scientists in Massachusetts had seeded a

cloud to make it rain, but the falling water had evaporated before it hit the ground.)

Although this was a good start to the program, as more experiments were done the results became very confusing. Nobody could predict exactly where the rain would fall. Furthermore, the special cold clouds, the only ones suitable for seeding, were rare. So, in 1983, after more than 30 years of experimenting, the official Australian rainmaking program was closed down.

Not everyone thought this was a good idea. Two CSIRO (Commonwealth Scientific and Industrial Research Organisation) scientists, Dr Taffy Bowen and Dr Keith Bigg, claimed, in 1985, that seeding clouds really did work, but over much larger areas and for longer periods of time than originally thought. For example, the rain might sometimes fall a few days later, not straightaway. By this time, the original cloud could be hundreds of kilometres away from where it had been seeded. So the effect of the seeding might not have been noticed. According to their analysis of the data, this is what did happen.

Even though the Australian rainmaking effort had stopped, other people kept trying to control the weather. The Soviets injected tiny particles of silver iodide or lead iodide directly into the clouds — with rockets. As the rockets passed through the cloud in some 45 seconds, they would burn a special chemical that was loaded with the iodide. In this instance, they were not really interested in making rain. They claimed that they could reduce the severity of hailstorms, by getting the ice pellets to fall sooner.

In recent times, there has been an upswing of interest in making rain.

Names of Cyclones – America

In America, for most of the last century, only the biggest cyclones were given names. But during World War II, weather could help or hinder the armed forces. So it became general practice for the United States Navy to name tropical cyclones in the South Pacific, an important area for America.

In 1950, America adopted the idea of calling major storms after the letters of the radio alphabet used by the military – Able, Baker, Charlie and so on. Around 1952, female names were added to the official list, but they were used only for really big and nasty storms. Some people thought this was a bit unfair!

Around 1979 meteorologists decided to use male and female names alternately. Just recently, there has been another change thanks to the very mixed population of America – Spanish and French names have been added. Typical cyclone names include Luis, Pablo, Allison and Phillipe. But a cyclone can change its name – if a cyclone starts in the Atlantic Ocean with the name Karl, and crosses over Mexico into the Pacific Ocean, there it could be renamed Emma. The first cyclone of a season is given a name beginning with A, the second one a name beginning with B, and so on. Male and female names are used alternately, but the letters Q, U, X, Y and Z are never used.

If a cyclone causes great destruction, then its name is 'retired' from the list of potential names and never used again. Nobody will ever get confused about Cyclone Tracy, because there was only one Cyclone Tracy (see box, *Cyclones – Big and Little*).

Names of Cyclones — Anywhere

A cyclone is a major storm that rotates around a central eye, and can be enormously destructive. But it is called a 'cyclone' only in the Indian and South Pacific Oceans.

In the western part of the North Pacific Ocean, they are called 'typhoons' — which comes from the Chinese word 'taifun', meaning 'great wind'. In the Philippines, the name is 'baguio' or 'baruio'. In America, they use the name 'hurricane', which comes from the West Indian word 'huracan' and means 'big wind'. In Haiti it is called a 'taino', while off the west coast of Mexico the name 'cordonazo' is used.

The state of Texas and Texas Tech have combined to run a rain-making program for the past 25 years. Worldwide, there are over 92 groups from 23 countries trying to make rain.

The current feeling is that scientists should be able to increase summer rain by 15%, and the mountain snowfall by 30%. But the US military think that they can do much better than this. A 1997 report (which talks about 'Project Popeye') from the Air War College in America is called *Weather as a Force Multiplier: Owning the Weather*. The American military are quite serious. In trying to control the weather, we're dealing with enormous amounts of energy. An average cyclone burns up about 100 billion kilowatts of power. In just 24 hours a cyclone that burns up power at this rate will use as much energy as a large industrialised country will in a whole year! If you're going to try to send a cyclone over the enemy, you want to make sure that you can control all that power. It would make a real mess if the cyclone turned back and rolled over you, instead of over the enemy!

Cyclones have enormous power. They range from Category 1 (winds over 120 kph) to Category 5 (winds over 250 kph). In 1988, Hurricane Gilbert had winds stronger than 350 kph. In 1969, Hurricane Camille in America created a huge tide, some 7.5 metres higher than usual. That tide flooded a lot of land. In Bangladesh, in 1970, one single cyclone killed 500,000 people.

Cyclones – Big and Little

Typhoon Tip, which occurred in the northwest Pacific Ocean, was one of the biggest cyclones ever recorded. On 12 October 1979, it had major winds reaching out some 1110 km from the eye, or centre, of the storm.

One of the smallest cyclones ever recorded was Cyclone Tracy – its winds reached out only 50 km from its centre. But it was very powerful!

On Christmas Eve 1974, it struck Darwin, killing over 50 people and causing massive destruction because it raged right over the middle of the city.

In May 1996, the Mongolian Army controlled the weather to put out a huge fire that was threatening their capital city, Ulan Bator. This fire was the culmination of three weeks of fires that had burnt 80,000 square kilometres of forest and pasture land, had already killed five people, and had already cost their economy $2.3 billion.

The Army fired special rainmaking shells into the heavy clouds over Ulan Bator. Within 20 minutes, a 15 cm snowfall began, which soon put out the fires!

This was a peaceful use of weather control. A Weather War would involve being able to send the right sort of clouds over the enemy, and make them dump their rain.

Bad weather can interfere with military operations. During the first two days of the Gulf War in 1991, the weather was so bad that the Allied Forces could not fly all their missions that were planned. Two hundred A-10 Warthog Ground Attack plane missions were planned for those first two days, but only 75 could be flown. More than half the F-117 Stealth Fighters had to abandon their missions, because the weather was so bad.

But imagine you could do more than dump rain on the enemy. Those who work in the field of weather control talk of setting off lightning bolts from thunderclouds to blast enemy aircraft by 'tickling the thunderclouds with laser beams'. And it

Military Weather

In 1274 and 1281, a Mongol battle fleet was sailing to invade Japan. But a typhoon sprang up and completely obliterated the Mongol fleet. The Japanese called this typhoon a 'kamikaze', or 'divine wind'.

would be devastating to the enemy if you could dump a cyclone on top of them!

Mark Twain was supposed to have said: *Everybody talks about the weather, but nobody does anything about it*. That's not true any more.

Rain-busting

Sometimes it's better to stop rain from falling if it can cause damage.

American storm experts did this in 2001. They used large military planes to sprinkle 4000 kg of water-absorbing powder over a cloud some 1600 metres long and some 4000 metres deep. This powder can absorb over 2000 times its own weight in water.

The cloud just literally disappeared. This technique might work on a single cloud — but stopping a 100-km storm front would be a different proposition.

Australian Torpedo and Monorail

Louis Brennan invented the 'Tin Fish' — the most dangerous creature in the oceans. It wasn't literally a fish made from tin — it was a torpedo.

Back in 1863, the word 'torpedo' didn't mean a tube full of explosive that raced through the water, hit its target and then exploded.

Back then, the word torpedo had two quite different meanings, each involving things going 'bang'.

One meaning for the word torpedo was a floating mine, full of high explosive, that would explode when a ship bumped into it. But a torpedo could also be a 'spar' torpedo. A spar torpedo was a charge of explosive tied onto the end of a long pole, or spar. The spar was tied onto the bow of a small launch. A volunteer in the launch would ram the high explosive (and the launch) into the enemy ship. It was a devastating weapon, but nobody wanted to volunteer to sail the launch!

An English engineer, Robert Whitehead, built the first self-propelled modern torpedo in 1866. It was hopelessly inaccurate as a weapon.

It was Louis Brennan, in Australia, who turned the torpedo into a devastating weapon that everybody feared.

In World War I and World War II, the torpedo was a terrible weapon. It destroyed more tonnage of ships than any other weapon, including bombs. Torpedoes were delivered from submarines, patrol torpedo boats, planes, destroyers and even light cruisers.

Louis Brennan was born in Ireland in 1852. When he was only nine years old, he and his parents moved to Melbourne. He worked as an apprentice for a watchmaker and then an engineer. By the tender age of 22 he had designed his torpedo.

His torpedo was very fast — even faster than the

Whitehead's Torpedo

In 1864 the Australian Navy approached Robert Whitehead and asked him to design and build a self-propelled boat that could be steered from where it was launched by long lines. He could not get this steering concept to work, and abandoned it to work on his own designs.

One of his designs was a torpedo, a cylinder about 4 metres long, 36 cm in diameter, and weighing about 140 kg — which included some 8 kg of dynamite at the front end. The power came from compressed air, which turned a single propeller. Although it did not have any system to steer it towards a target, or to bring it back on course if it turned to one side, it did have a device to measure its depth — an automatic mechanism operated horizontal wings to keep it at the correct depth. It had a top speed of only 11 kph, and a range of about 650 metres.

By 1895, Whitehead had improved his torpedo by installing a gyroscope. If the torpedo began to go off course, the gyroscope would operate vertical wings to bring it back on course.

But his torpedo was not as accurate, or as fast, as the Brennan Torpedo.

ships of the day. It could be steered onto its target by remote control. It didn't even carry its own fuel — it was powered from the launching station. It was designed to protect military harbours and naval forts on land from attack by enemy ships.

Brennan designed his torpedo, but needed cash to build it. For some reason, the Victorian Government thought that Melbourne might be an attractive target for aggressive European nations. So they gave him £700 ($1400) to build a working model of his torpedo. It was successfully tested in Hobson's Bay, Melbourne, on 21 March 1897. This was the first time in history that a weapon had been successfully guided right onto its target!

The torpedo 'excited wonder and approbation' from the politicians, journalists and military officers who were watching the test.

The next year Brennan went to London to show off his invention. The Royal Engineers at Chatham

Brennan's torpedo

were so impressed with it that Brennan was awarded £5000 immediately, and another £1000 per year while he improved his design.

Brennan's torpedo was driven by two propellers. They rotated in opposite directions. Each propeller was attached to a steel drum. Wrapped around each drum were several kilometres of very skinny, super-strong, high-tensile steel wire. All of this was in the body of the torpedo.

The two wires came out of the torpedo and were connected to a launching station back on the shore. The wires were pulled out of the torpedo by a pair of 20-horsepower steam engines at the launching station.

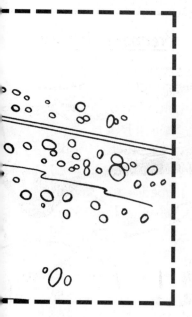

It sounds impossible to make a machine travel forward by pulling on it. But you can try it with a reel of cotton. Put the cotton reel on the ground, with the cotton thread coming towards you on the bottom side of the reel, not the top side. Then pull on this cotton and the reel will move away from you.

Because there were two propellers, there were also two drums, two wires and two steam engines. The

Launching Officer was in a high tower, with a set of high-powered binoculars, watching the speeding torpedo. To steer the weapon all he had to do was to speed up or slow down one of the steam engines.

The Royal Navy was so impressed with Brennan's torpedo that they paid him £110,000 — an enormous sum of money in those days. They thought it was a brilliant weapon.

Not only could it zip through the water at up to 50 kph, it also had a range of 2 km. It could be very accurately steered by the operator all the way through that 2-km range. This was at a time when the other available torpedoes could travel at only half that speed, and would nearly always miss if the target were further away than 350 metres.

In one demonstration, Brennan's torpedo was aimed at the rather odd target of a floating basket of fruit, some 2 km away. Not only could the Brennan Torpedo hit it straight on, it could even go in a wide circle and attack from the other side!

The Brennan Torpedo was 7.3 metres long, weighed 3.5 tonnes and carried 100 kg of explosives.

The body of the Brennan Torpedo was slightly elliptical, or egg-shaped — 60 cm wide and 76 cm high. This had the advantage of stopping the torpedo from rolling.

It was never used on the high seas, only close to shore, and was stored on land. Just like an emergency lifeboat, when it was needed it ran down rails until it hit the water. It would then run about 3.3 metres beneath the surface.

There is a spectacular photograph in the Royal Engineers Museum at Chatham, in England. This shows

The 'Invisible' Inventor

Louis Brennan was an 'invisible' inventor. He invented a torpedo that was kept as secret as possible and never used in combat, and a helicopter that only the military ever saw fly.

One reason why this was so was because of his involvement with the military – they wanted to keep his inventions to themselves.

He had worked on the torpedo with the brilliant William Charles Kernot from Melbourne University. He intended to show it off at the Melbourne International Exhibition in 1880. But his first demonstration was so impressive that he and his plans and models were quickly whisked off to England, before the Exhibition happened.

His helicopter was also kept under military secrecy. The British Government asked Brennan to work on a helicopter. They wanted it to fly at 90 kph, and climb to 700 metres. Brennan worked at Farnborough, in England. We do know that his helicopter apparently fulfilled the requirements; in a book about Brennan, there is a black and white photo of his helicopter hovering outdoors in an open field.

a Brennan Torpedo slamming into a target ship, the SS *Monarch*, which was being towed at 25 kph. This museum also has the only known surviving Brennan Torpedo in existence.

Even today, there is still one mystery left about the Brennan Torpedo — how it managed to maintain a steady cruising depth, staying at the same distance under the surface of the water, as it zipped towards its target.

The Brennan Torpedo became the standard way of defending harbours and naval installations throughout the British Empire — from Dover to Gibraltar to Singapore. For 20 years, from 1885 to 1905, it was the only way to defend a British harbour. In fact, it was so important to the British Navy that the War Office refused to sell a dozen to the Victorian Government. And Victoria had given the very first support and cash to that Australian invention!

None of Brennan's other inventions made him so much money. He invented a 'biograph' — a machine that turned a series of still photographs into moving pictures. He also invented mincing machines, soldering rods, food packers, wool clippers and chicken incubators.

He created a small, hand-held, silent typewriter that used only five characters. This meant that every character could be typed with the fingers of one hand. It has recently reappeared as the 'Microwriter'.

His 'Ascent of Stairs' machine had a seat attached to a rail, and could take disabled people up a set of stairs.

Brennan also invented the monorail to provide fast, cheap transport for Australia. Australia has a small population that mostly hugs the coast, huge distances between towns, and patches of hilly countryside. These factors make a transport system expensive to operate.

He invented a *true* monorail, a railway system with one rail — 'mono' means 'one'. Modern monorails have two or more rails, but run on a single post. So they should really be called monoposts, not monorails. His system worked on just a single steel cable, strung from post to post, or hilltop to hilltop. His monorail locomotive could run on a single rail because it was stabilised by a gyroscope — a heavy spinning wheel.

If you have ever spun a spinning top, you know it doesn't like to change direction. If you make it much heavier and spin it much faster, the gyroscopic force is large enough to stop even a heavy locomotive from tipping over.

Brennan's monorail was demonstrated to the Royal Society in 1907. The newspapers of the day started calling it a 'Spinning Top Railway' or the 'Automatic Blondin Train'. (Blondin was a famous tightrope walker of the 19th century who crossed Niagara Falls on a tightrope. He did this in many

41

Brennan's Monorail

different ways — carrying a man on his back, bouncing in a sack, trembling on tall stilts, pushing a wheelbarrow and even blindfolded!)

Brennan's monorail was a brilliant idea. It was cheap to build because it had only one rail, not two. One rail was also much quieter than two. You didn't need to build expensive bridges or supports — you could simply string a steel cable from hilltop to hilltop. The monorail locomotive could take very sharp corners by leaning into them, just like riders on motorbikes have to do.

But it didn't become a success.

The Indian, Australian and British Governments were all interested but wouldn't advance any money. Perhaps they thought the general public would not have any confidence in one rail — they would want two rails.

Even today, the monorails in Japan, America and Sydney are not true monorails. The carriages rest on a railway line that has between two and four rails. But a modern monorail still has the advantage that it can go where it likes — between tall buildings and over roads. Sometimes monorails can even go into buildings to pick up passengers.

Brennan's talents were enormous — he also worked on helicopters. (Leonardo da Vinci designed the first helicopter way back in 1490. Da Vinci had experimented with large propellers made of starched linen. He had found that: *if this instrument*

Brennan's Gyrocar

returns swiftly, the said screw will make its spiral in the air and will rise high. But the first helicopter flight was several centuries later, in 1907.)

Over a period of about five years, 1915 to 1925, Brennan worked on improvements to helicopter design. Unfortunately, his very sophisticated machine was apparently destroyed in a crash in 1925.

But Brennan would not stop working and at the age of 74 he began developing a two-wheeled

'Gyrocar'.

However, the conventional car manufacturers were selling all of the four-wheeled cars that they could make, and didn't want to know about a two-wheeled car. Brennan kept on working on cars until he died in Switzerland in 1932 — sadly, knocked down and killed by a car.

Waterbag and Coolgardie Safe

If you ever get a chance to travel through the Australian outback, you'll see lots of things. One of them will definitely be the waterbag hanging off the front of cars and trucks. Waterbags are made of canvas. They're a great way for travellers to carry drinking water.

Waterbags work like a refrigerator — they turn warm water into cool water.

The water cools down because of evaporation. Evaporation happens when tiny particles of a liquid (called molecules) turn into a gas. Water starts off as a liquid, but after you heat it up it turns into a gas called steam. Water boils at 100°C, but evaporation can happen at much lower temperatures (like at 37°C, the temperature inside your mouth).

anvas might seem like a strange material to make waterbags out of, because it isn't waterproof. When you fill canvas bags water seeps through to the outside. This water on the outside of the canvas bag then evaporates — and it takes energy to make this happen. All of this energy comes from the water left behind in the bag. After the warmer, faster molecules have evaporated away, the water inside the waterbag has less energy — the molecules are moving slowly and, therefore, the water is colder. That's how canvas waterbags can make the water inside cool down.

If you drive around with a waterbag on the front of your car, the moving air will carry away more of the water molecules from the outside of the waterbag. So when you are moving you will lose more water from your waterbag than when you are still — but the water left behind in the waterbag will be colder.

The waterbag was introduced to Europeans by Major Thomas Mitchell. He was a Surveyor-General of New South Wales and an explorer. He suddenly realised how beautiful waterbags were on his fourth major expedition in 1846, while he was exploring southwestern Queensland. At that time, European travellers carried water in wooden kegs. He happened to see some Aborigines carrying water in bags made of kangaroo skin. He realised that, full or empty, bags were much easier to carry than wooden kegs.

Major Thomas Mitchell – Wild Man and Writer

By 1851, Mitchell was Sir Thomas Mitchell. But it didn't make his manners any better! He actually fought a duel in Centennial Park with Sir Stuart Donaldson, the first Premier of New South Wales.

Donaldson didn't believe the figures in the expense accounts issued by Mitchell's department – and he said so in public. In return, Mitchell called Donaldson a liar.

In their duel, Mitchell and Donaldson each fired three shots. Nobody was hurt, but Donaldson's top hat had a hole blown through it!

But Mitchell was not just a macho man – he was also an author. He wrote about military matters and how to grow olives and vines, and translated an epic Portuguese poem.

Major Mitchell decided to improve on the kangaroo skin design, but for a while he actually made them worse! He sewed together some pieces of canvas to make a bag. To stop the water leaking out, he greased the canvas with melted tallow. (Tallow is a hard fat that comes from sheep.) The tallow did make the canvas watertight — but it also made the water taste really bad!

So he started again and made a new lot of canvas bags. This time, he didn't grease them with

waterbag

Waterbags are very handy to have when travelling in the outback.

tallow. The water tasted terrific! And to his surprise, once the bag got completely wet it didn't drip water everywhere — thanks to surface tension, which is a force unique to liquids that makes the surface different from the bulk of the liquid. (Surface tension is why rain comes down as drops, all neatly rolled up, not as a continuous stream.) And because the bag was wet, the water on the outside could evaporate, cooling the water inside the bag down.

There's a statue starring the waterbag in Kalgoorlie in Western Australia. It shows Patrick Hannan sharing water from his waterbag. (He was a generous man.) Patrick is the man who discovered the Kalgoorlie goldfields. The story goes that he picked up a stone to throw at a crow and, to his surprise, saw that the stone was actually a gold nugget. Even though more than one billion dollars' worth of gold was taken out of the ground, Hannan died penniless in 1925.

The 'Coolgardie safe', like the waterbag, uses evaporating water to keep things cool inside it. In the gold rush of the 1890s, thousands of prospectors flocked to Coolgardie in Western Australia — not far from Kalgoorlie.

Coolgardie was hot and dusty, and the few hundred kilometres to the nearest civilisation took at least eight days. Food went bad very quickly in the desert heat.

Coolgardie safe

A fellow called A.P. McCormick thought up the Coolgardie safe, which works like a refrigerator but runs on water. He made it using local materials.

Firstly, he put all of his food into a wooden box. Then he wrapped it up with a wet hessian bag. Not only did the wet bag keep the food inside the box cool, but it also kept the flies and the dust off.

Unfortunately, the heat dried out the wet bag very quickly, so McCormick worked out a way to keep the bag wet. He put a tray on top of the box, and filled the tray with water. Then he put some strips of flannel into the water, and draped them down over the box.

The flannel acted like a wick, and carried the water from the tray to the hessian bag. The tray had to be filled only a few times each day.

Of course, the safe would cool the food better if it were in the shade and in a breeze, so it was often

Try Evaporation Now!

You can try this right now — put your finger into your mouth, and get it nice and wet. Then, take your finger out of your mouth and blow on it. You'll feel your finger get cooler!

This is a two-part process — getting your finger wet, and then blowing on it.

When your finger is wet, some of the water molecules leave your finger to fly off into the air. Normally, water likes to stay all stuck together because of surface tension. You need energy to make water molecules let go of each other. If you're boiling water, this energy comes from the heat (and with the waterbag the energy came from the water inside the bag). When your finger is wet, the energy comes from your finger. So your finger ends up with less energy. Less energy means less heat, so that's why wetting your finger makes it a bit colder.

Now, when the molecules jump off your wet finger, the law of averages means that about half of them jump right back on again! The other half move further away. If all of them jumped back onto your finger, the temperature wouldn't change. If none of them jumped back onto your finger, the temperature would drop a lot. By blowing on your wet finger more of these floating water molecules are pushed away. So less of them will be around to jump back on your finger. This leads to a colder temperature.

So, getting your finger wet cools it down a bit, and blowing on it cools it down even more.

put out on the verandah or under a tree. The Coolgardie safe worked so well that soon factories started making the safe with a water tray built into the top, a wooden frame, a hessian bag wrapped around the outside, shelves, a door and even little legs. And if you stood the legs of the safe in bowls of water, ants couldn't get at the nice cool food.

It may have had nothing to do with his invention, but McCormick was later Mayor of Coolgardie, from 1908 to 1909.

Refrigeration

The invention of refrigeration has given us many things, including refrigerated transport, blood banks, sperm banks, air conditioning in houses and cars, open-heart surgery and ice cream!

Refrigeration made Australia so wealthy that by the turn of the century we had the highest living standard on the entire planet! And it all happened because a boy went fishing with his father.

In 1867, Australia had more food (sheep running around paddocks!) than it could eat, while Europe had too little food. Unfortunately, there was no easy way that the Europeans could eat those millions of surplus Australian sheep. It was not economic to send live animals on a long sea voyage — few would survive. Canned meat was expensive and, besides, it was unpopular.

All that Australian farmers could do was to boil the meat down to make tallow (used for candles and soap) and mash up the blood and bone (for fertiliser). So, while only wealthy Europeans could eat meat, at least everybody else could wash their hands with cheap soap, after putting cheap fertiliser on their crops.

In 1867, there was no easy way to preserve foods.

Foods spoil because of a whole bunch of different factors. These include living creatures such as bacteria and fungi, and natural chemicals in the food called enzymes (you've probably heard of them in washing powder — they 'eat' stains!). At sub-zero

Refrigeration has given us ...

refrigerated trucks   sperm banks   air conditioning

Cooling the Deepest Mine

According to *The Guinness Book of Records*, the deepest mine in the world is the Western Deep Levels gold mine at Carletonville, in South Africa. This mine is 3777 metres deep. As you go underground, it rapidly gets hotter. So, to make it possible for humans to work underground, this mine has enough refrigeration capacity to make over 40,000 tonnes of ice each day!

temperatures, the bacteria and fungi go to sleep and don't multiply any more. The enzymes need to be stored at these extremely low temperatures too, or they will keep attacking the food so that it goes bad.

The ancient Greeks and Romans could preserve food with ice taken from the high mountains. The wealthy would have a pit dug in their garden, which they would fill with ice, and then cover with wood and straw. This method is still used in some parts of the world.

Naturally occurring ice is one of the oldest ways to preserve food for up to two months. In 1806, a 21-year-old American, Frederick Tudor, used saws to cut ice from the frozen ponds of Boston. He shipped 130 tonnes of ice to the hot, tropical island of Martinique, by using straw, wood shavings and blankets to keep the ice cold. He developed insulating techniques so that he would only lose up to 8% of his ice over an entire hot summer, and by 1840 he was exporting ice all over the world. Successful Australian gold prospectors could drink beer cooled by this Boston ice. The 19th-century clipper ships made a good living shifting ice, but it was difficult to handle and load and it was still too expensive for the general public.

Food Poisoning

When you cool some foods, you don't actually *kill* the bacteria. They just go to sleep for as long as they are kept cold. If the food warms up again, they wake up and start multiplying.

But the bacteria that live in some of the soft cheeses don't multiply very well unless you give them another period of cooling down. So, if you take your soft cheeses in and out of the fridge often, you're increasing your chances of getting poisoned by the bacteria in them.

James Harrison was a journalist and a politician, but he also built the first practical refrigerator. He was born in Scotland, the son of a salmon fisherman. As a child, he saw his father storing freshly caught salmon using imported American ice.

He became apprenticed to a printer, and in 1837, at the age of 22, he was given the job of delivering

Tinned Food

The idea of putting food in small cans was invented about two centuries ago. In 1795, the French Government set up a competition to provide safe food supplies for its troops. Nicolas Appert came up with the idea of putting the food into a can and sealing it. Immediately after they sealed the food into the can, they cooked it in the same can. This saved on the extra labour of shifting the cooked food into the can. It also meant that no more bacteria or fungi could get into the can. The high temperatures of the cooking killed all the bacteria and fungi, so that afterwards they could store the can at room temperature. The higher the temperature, the more bacteria die. It turns out that every time you increase the temperature by another 10°C, 10 times more bacteria die from the heat. By the time you get to over 115°C, you have killed all the bacteria.

However, some of the natural chemicals in the food might still be able to spoil the food. But at sub-zero temperatures, canned food in the Antarctic has remained perfectly edible after 50 years! These are the instructions on one of the cans that Sir William Parry carried with him to the Arctic in 1824: *Cut around the top with a chisel and hammer.*

The can was made from thick iron, and weighed about half a kilogram! The silly thing is that the can-opener wasn't invented at the same time as the can! The can-opener was invented (probably) in the 1870s, 80 years after the invention of the can.

printing equipment to Sydney. He decided to stay in Australia. In 1840, he went to Geelong to set up the *Geelong Advertiser*, the oldest morning newspaper in Victoria. But he still remembered his father and the salmon stored in the ice, and he still had his dream of cheap, cold storage.

He had been using ether in his printing press to clean the type used for printing. He noticed that as the ether evaporated into the air, it made the type very cold. As ether evaporates and expands, it cools down. In fact, as any gas expands it cools down.

You can feel temperature changes by blowing air onto the palm of your hand. If you open your mouth widely and blow onto the palm of your hand it will get warm. But try it after closing your mouth down into a very small hole. The air is compressed, or squashed, to get through the small hole, and then it expands, which uses energy. While it is still expanding, it hits your hand. The palm of your hand feels cold! This is the basic principle of refrigeration.

Harrison twisted some hollow pipe into the shape of a coil. The coil had many turns. Then he put some ether at high pressure into a tank, which was connected to the coil. When he let the ether expand into the hollow coil, it got very cold. And when he put the coil into a barrel of water, the water turned into ice. He did his experiments in a small cave on the bank of the Barwon River in Geelong. But the trouble with ether is that the smallest spark will make it explode. In fact, he was once badly injured by such an explosion.

By 1857, though, he had built his ether refrigerator, and was turning out 3 tonnes of ice per day from a small factory on the Barwon River. He would put a flower, or an entire fish, into a block of ice and present it to a visitor. By 1858, his artificial ice had been used to reduce fevers, and so save lives. Unfortunately, the local people did not like his artificial ice — it wasn't 'natural'. So he decided to move to Melbourne.

By 1859, his Melbourne factory was turning out 10 tonnes of ice per day. He thought that people in the 'big smoke' would be less prejudiced — but still he could not sell enough of his ice. It had tiny bubbles in it, while the ice cut from ponds in America was perfectly clear.

Harrison had enough energy and talent to be both a topnotch inventor and a full-time journalist. In fact, he was good enough to become editor of the *Age*, one of the most respected newspapers in Australia. So he wasn't going to give up easily.

In 1873, he froze some meat at the Victorian Exhibition in Melbourne. When the meat was defrosted and cooked after 97 days, it still tasted perfectly fresh. One of the guests at the public banquet said: 'Equal to newly killed meat, and full of flavour.' For this feat Harrison won a gold medal. He was now ready to start sending meat overseas.

Snap Freezing

Why does frozen food not taste the same as when it was fresh? Charles Birdseye discovered part of the answer. In the early 1920s, he was on a hunting trip in Labrador (the northeastern part of Canada). He noticed that fish that were frozen very rapidly kept their fresh taste for many months.

The reason for this was discovered accidentally by Max Planck, a German quantum physicist.

When a liquid freezes, crystals are formed. Planck found out that for each liquid there is a certain temperature range in which very large crystals are formed. For water, this range is between -4°C and -0.5°C.

When food is cooled slowly, and spends a lot of time between these temperatures, large crystals are formed. These crystals then pierce the walls of the cells that make up food. The food looks fine, so long as it stays frozen. But when you thaw the food, the water in the cells runs out through the holes in the cell walls and the food becomes mushy and horrible.

Charles Birdseye realised that the secret was to take the food through this tricky temperature range in minutes, not hours. This would mean that the large crystals wouldn't get a chance to form.

Nowadays, much food is snap frozen, either by a blast of air at -40°C, or a spray of liquid at -29°C.

A few months later, he shipped 25 tonnes of prime beef to London on the *Norfolk*. However, for a number of reasons, the meat was rotten and unfit to be eaten when it arrived: it had been handled very roughly while it was being loaded, the journey was very rough and very long, the freezing machinery could not be run continuously, and none of the crew really knew how to work the machinery properly. Harrison was financially ruined.

In 1877, another team of inventors built refrigeration equipment into another ship, the *Northam*. Thomas Sutcliffe Mort, who helped to found the company Goldsbrough Mort, spent £100,000 on this project. (Mort did many great things. He founded Australia's first heavy engineering works to make ships and locomotives. He also set up the first profit-sharing operation in Australia. The employees actually owned shares in the company. As the company became wealthy, so did the workers.)

For this refrigeration project, Mort teamed up with a Frenchman, Eugene Nicolle. Nicolle used the same principles as Harrison had, but instead of ether he used ammonia. Ammonia is not explosive. Unfortunately, though, the rebuilt refrigeration equipment on the *Northam* couldn't be made to work properly by the time the ship had to sail.

On 29 November 1879, the *Strathleven*, another newly refrigerated ship, set sail from Sydney Harbour with 40 tonnes of beef and mutton. It arrived in London on 2 February 1880. The meat

History of Artificial Refrigeration

In 1784, William Cullen at the University of Glasgow demonstrated what is probably the very first known case of artificial refrigeration, or cooling. He showed that when ether evaporates, it cools down. However, he did not actually design or build a working refrigerator.

In 1805, Oliver Evans in America designed a refrigeration machine, but did not actually build it. In 1834, Jacob Perkins, an American engineer living in London, took out a patent on one of the first useful machines that could make ice. In 1844, an American doctor, John Gorrie, built a machine to cool sickrooms. His main aim was to provide comfort to victims of yellow fever, who were suffering both from the fever and from the heat of summertime Florida. In 1856, another American, Alexander C. Twinning, actually started using his cooling machines to make money. In the same year, the Australian James Harrison made his refrigerators, using ether, to cool meat and beer. In 1858, in France, Ferdinand P.A. Carré built a refrigerator that used liquid ammonia.

In 1879, an Australian shipment of frozen meat was successfully sent to England. In 1881, in Chicago, Gustavus F. Swift designed and built a refrigerator railway car that carried frozen meat. By the year 1910, people understood how to make refrigerators. In America, refrigerator sales were 10,000 in 1920, 75,000 in 1925 and 800,000 in 1929!

arrived in perfect condition. This was the first international exportation of frozen meat.

The *Strathleven* was funded by a Sydney group headed by Andrew McIlwraith. A new industry had been created — the exporting of perishable food. Not just beef, mutton and lamb, but also butter and cheese could be sent to anywhere on our planet. By 1900, a million frozen carcasses were being sent to England each year.

In 1967, the Australian Institute of Refrigeration said that James Harrison was 'unquestionably the practical inventor of commercial refrigeration'. On his gravestone is written: *One soweth, another reapeth.*

Landing Aircraft Safely

The most dangerous part of any aeroplane journey is not when you're flying at full speed. The most dangerous part of any flight is when your plane is moving fairly slowly and when it's close to the ground — in other words, takeoff and landing. That's when 40% of plane accidents happen. (But a plane is much safer than a car when you compare the distance each travels.)

So there has always been a need to help planes land safely — especially in bad weather, such as heavy rain or fog.

One of the early landing systems was invented in the 1940s. The Instrument Landing System (ILS) (which later evolved into the Microwave Landing System or MLS) uses two radio transmitters set up near a runway or landing strip. Each transmitter puts out a separate radio beam.

One radio beam looks like an open fan lying on its back, tilted at 3° above the ground. The second beam looks like an open fan held vertically, and runs out in a straight line from the centre of the runway. The two beams cross each other at right angles.

The 'glide path' is where these two beams cross over each other, and there is only one glide path for each runway. The glide path is an invisible, straight radio 'road' in the sky. It's about 15 km long and tilted up at 3°. The aircraft has a special radio receiver to pick up these beams. The pilots of the plane then travel, as accurately as possible, down the glide path, all the way to the centre of the runway. The planes are like cars spread out on a very long, straight road. They are a few kilometres apart.

The ILS was a great invention and it became very popular. By the mid–1980s, 623 airports in America and another 750 outside America were using the ILS.

But as plane flight became cheaper and more popular, problems began to emerge. The big problem with the ILS is in having only one glide path. This means that a slow propeller plane can hold up a long queue of faster jets. The longer that a plane is in the air, the more fuel that it uses. This is wasteful.

The ILS has a few other problems. The glide path is very shallow (only 3°), so the plane spends a lot of time at lower altitudes, even though it is safer for it to stay at a higher altitude and speed. Also, the path is very straight and narrow. This means that the pilot has to be very accurate and it also means that the plane may end up flying over hospitals, schools or houses. This is a big problem.

Maybe we should get planes to fly over industrial areas — but that's not fair either. Why should workers in such areas, who are already at risk from the noise around them, be blasted with even more noise? Noise is a problem that affects all of us — and usually, it's better to fix a problem at the source. One solution might be to use more modern, quieter planes — but airlines will wait for the older planes to wear out first!

There is something that would be a lot better than a single, straight glide path — and that is a

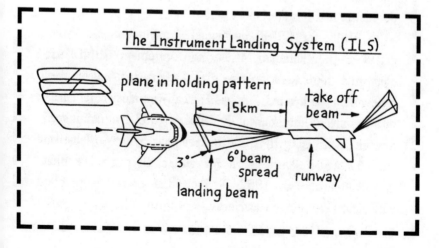

The Instrument Landing System (ILS)

plane in holding pattern

15km

take off beam →

3°

6° beam spread

landing beam

runway

bunch of curved glide paths in the sky. This would allow slow, medium and fast planes to each travel on their own separate glide path.

In 1972, the ICAO (International Civil Aviation Organisation) set up a competition for a better aircraft landing system. The guidelines for the competition stated that the planes had to know exactly where they were at all times. They would fly down a giant invisible 'pyramid' made of radio waves. The pyramid would be lying on one side and have its point on the centre of the runway. It would stretch out 40° on each side of the runway, reach

Flying and Not Getting Lost

In the early days of flying it was really easy for pilots to get lost, even when they had clear sky. It was even easier to get lost in bad weather, or at night.

In 1945, the CSIRO developed a navigation aid system called DME (Distance Measuring Equipment). DME used electronic equipment on the plane which listened to radio beacons on the ground – it was basically an electronic version of a system of lighthouses. By January 1947, two commercial aircraft were using DME on their regular Sydney–Melbourne run. By 1953, there were 95 automatic ground stations across Australia. By 1957, all Australian aircraft were fitted with Australian-made receivers.

Australian Radio Waves Found Invading Fleet of Planes

Australian scientists have had lots of experience with radio waves and microwaves. In 1940 we had already developed our own radar system, which worked on radio waves. It could find ships 40 km out at sea.

Spurred on by defence needs during World War II, in 1941 this system was modified by Jack Piddington and his group of physicists. They wanted to detect enemy aircraft. The system was set up at Dover Heights, just a few kilometres from Bondi Beach. On its first trial, it detected aircraft 105 km out at sea.

One of the first working models was pulled to pieces and sent to Darwin in February of 1942. By a terrible coincidence, it was still being installed when the Japanese bombed Darwin on the morning of 19 February. This was a national emergency! Jack Piddington and his team immediately flew to Darwin. They managed to get the system working by the morning of 22 February.

The very first thing that they detected was another Japanese bombing force! The scientists immediately passed this information to the military. The Japanese bombers did not get closer than 32 km to the coastline, because fighter planes had been sent out in time.

During World War II, the Division of Radio Physics at the CSIRO developed more that 20 different types of radar.

upward at 20° into the sky, and reach out 30 nautical miles (56 km) away from the runway.

Planes had to be able to do a perfect landing in any weather, even in practically zero visibility. The system had to be able to monitor several planes at the same time and the planes had to be able to fly down a glide path of any shape, from any direction. This meant that planes could avoid residential areas. For safety, the pilots also had to be able to land without using the plane's radio altimeter (which measures the height above the ground). Fast planes would enter the system, say, 30 km from the runway, while slow planes could enter at 10 km. The system could let through three fast planes, then one slow plane, and so on. This meant that fast planes would not be held up by slow planes.

By 1974, the ICAO had decided to use a technique proposed by an Australian team. Dr Paul Wild, the Head of the CSIRO Division of Radio Physics (and, later, Chairman of the CSIRO), was the head of this team. Their design used two moving beams of microwave energy, not two fixed beams of radio energy. These microwaves are very similar to the microwaves in your microwave oven. That's why it was called the Microwave Landing System, or MLS. The microwaves swept back and forth, and up and down very fast indeed — up to 40 times per second. The planes would measure the time delay, or interval, between when two sweeps of the beams hit them, and then work out where they were. (The MLS was also called by two other names: TRSB, for Time Reference Scanning Beam, or INTERSCAN, for INTERval SCANning.)

By 1975, Dr Wild and his team had designed, built and installed an experimental Interscan system at Melbourne airport. It was far more accurate than anyone had hoped for. The pilot landed his plane only 60 cm from the centre of the runway!

But the ICAO also wanted the system to be tested in America. The scientists packed up all their equipment and flew to Atlantic City, New Jersey. They bolted their special Interscan receiver onto a lump of wood. This wood was then screwed to the floor of a DC-6.

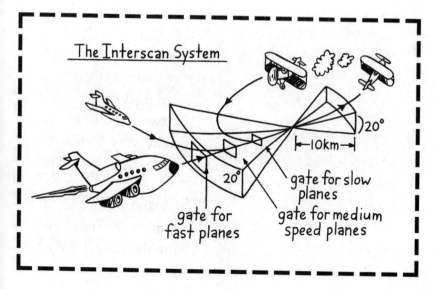

It worked well for six months — so well, in fact, that the ICAO decided that this idea of scanning the fan-shaped beam to the left and the right of the incoming plane was the best technique available. The scientists

The Famous Dr Wild

Today, Dr Wild is so famous that the central site for the giant $32 million Australia Telescope has been named the Paul Wild Observatory.

The Australia Telescope is the name for a lot of separate, small telescopes which together act like a super-giant radio telescope. They are all radio telescopes, which use big metal dishes, not optical telescopes which have glass mirrors, and are scattered over an area of 300 km. The Australia Telescope has six 22-metre radio telescopes at Culgoora, one 22-metre radio telescope at Siding Spring, and the giant 65-metre radio telescope at Parkes. Because it is so big, it is able to see very small objects in space.

But even before the 1970s Dr Wild had come up with several inventions.

In the 1940s, scientists discovered that the sun gave out not just light energy, but radio energy also. In 1949, Dr Wild set up one of the first radio telescopes in the world near the Blue Mountains, west of Sydney. He used it to look at the sun. He classified the different types of radio energy that our sun emitted and this method of classification is now accepted around the world. He then invented another machine for looking at radio waves, or energy, coming from the sun – a radio-heliograph. It has 96 separate antennae, and is located at Culgoora. It photographs the sun once every second, so you can see sudden, rapid changes as they actually happen.

He also invented the world's first radio-spectrograph, which shows the whole radio-frequency spectrum at the same time. It works just like a rainbow, showing you all the colours of light at once – each water droplet in the air breaks up white light into red, orange, yellow, green, blue, indigo and violet, which we see as the rainbow.

and engineers then flew back to Australia to show it off to fellow Australians. They installed all the necessary electronic equipment in a plane, and finally the Big Day of the Australian demonstration arrived. The plane rolled down the runway and took off. Once they were in the air, they began to test the equipment. But when they switched it on, it would not work!

As the plane flew in circles in the sky, the scientists pulled the equipment to pieces, desperately looking for a 'bug' in the machine. But the *bug* was an *animal*. A tiny field mouse had sneaked onto the plane and hidden inside the equipment! It had made a little nest deep inside, where it was nice and warm. They removed the mouse, cleaned up the equipment, and the Interscan receiver worked perfectly.

Somewhere deep inside the Interscan receiver...

An Australian company, called Interscan, was set up and combined with an American company. A few Interscan systems were installed in Australia and other parts of the world.

Interscan was operating so well by 1990 that the ICAO decided it would be the official standard landing system that all airports in the world would use.

By 1994, new technology made them change their minds again. This new technology is known as the Global Positioning System, or GPS.

Twenty-one satellites, orbiting the earth at a distance of 20,200 km, send microwave signals down to the ground. The GPS 'listens' to these microwaves and it will tell you, on a screen, where you are — anywhere on the earth.

The standard GPS, a favourite of bushwalkers and boat owners, is quite accurate. Most of the time, it will be accurate to within 5 to 15 metres (the width of a house).

Cheap hand-held GPS units are quite accurate — and very good value for money. You can buy, for around $250, a GPS unit that is the size of a mobile phone. The GPS equipment for planes is much more expensive *and* much more accurate — to within a few metres.

The first country in the world to use the GPS as their main landing and navigation system was the tiny island nation of Fiji, in 1993.

Fiji is a collection of some 300 to 800 islands over 2000 km north of New Zealand. The total population of about 750,000 lives on only 100 of these islands. It would have been too expensive to install the ILS or MLS at all the tiny airports on Fijian islands scattered across 1.6 million square kilometres of the South Pacific Ocean. It was much cheaper to simply install GPS units on the planes.

Since then, GPS units have become cheaper and more accurate. This is why it is the currently preferred system for landing aircraft safely.

Bionic Ear

The first successful bionic ear was developed by a team of Australian scientists led by Graeme Clark back in the 1970s. Graeme Clark invented the bionic ear because his father was deaf.

Life as a deaf person isn't easy. Sure, there's sign language and lip-reading, but it's still impossible to talk on the telephone!

People have been designing and building hearing aids for centuries. The most basic hearing aid is a hand held behind an ear in a cup shape to focus the sound waves into one point, to catch more sound. The important things are that the hand is larger than the ear and that it is kept curved.

Beethoven did his listening with his teeth, not his hands. Before he became totally deaf, he would clench a pencil between his teeth and hold it against the top of the piano. With partial hearing he could still *feel* the sound vibrations with his teeth. He even hit the keys so hard, trying to make the music louder to hear it more easily, that he regularly destroyed pianos.

John VI (1767–1826), who was the King of Portugal from 1816 to 1826, had probably the biggest hearing aid ever made — a special throne. The throne had lion heads at the end of hollow armrests. The lion mouths were open wide. The person speaking to the King would come and kneel in front of the chair and speak into a lion mouth. The sound travelled up the hollow armrest and through a pipe in the back of the chair that led directly into the King's ear. This hearing aid was specialised; it wouldn't be much good to anyone else, unless they had a throne and were prepared to sit around on it all day! So, manufacturers gradually tried to make hearing aids that were small and portable.

At first, hearing aids were very big. Trumpets with wide mouths were used to help collect more sound for the ear. Probably the very first trumpets were made from animal horns or tusks thousands of years ago. But people were embarrassed about being deaf so, as hearing aids became smaller, people tried to disguise them in all sorts of weird ways! They hid

their hearing aids in hats, bonnets, walking sticks, beards, fans and even tiaras.

Alexander Graham Bell tried very hard to invent a hearing aid. His work got sidetracked a bit when he actually ended up inventing the telephone. But others used his ideas to make better hearing aids.

Bell's brilliant idea was to turn sound energy into electrical energy. Then he would take the electrical energy and amplify it. Finally, the electrical energy would be turned back into a louder sound, which would be easier to hear.

However, the technology needed to make an *electronic* hearing aid was not invented until early in the 20th century. The first electronic hearing aids used amplifiers, which needed valves (also called tubes). They were bulky and used up lots of power. These hearing aids were powered by batteries, which, in the 1920s, were also very big and heavy. In 1923, a hearing aid was the size of a small suitcase and weighed 7 kg! By the 1930s, smaller valves brought the electronic hearing aid down to the size of a camera and the weight down to 2 kg. It was when transistor circuits were introduced in the 1950s that it became possible to make tiny hearing devices. The transistors were much smaller than valves and could run off smaller batteries.

But the real revolution happened in the 1970s, when Professor Graeme Clark and his team in Melbourne developed a bionic ear. They were

How the Human Ear Works

The human ear has three parts.

First, there is the outer ear. This is the part that you can see. It's full of air. It catches the sounds and sends them down the auditory canal to the eardrum. The eardrum vibrates.

The second part is the middle ear. In it are the smallest bones in the whole body, and the smallest joints. These bones connect the eardrum to a window on the outside of the inner ear. The bones are a set of levers that operate one after the other. They multiply the size of the back-and-forth movement of the eardrum by 22 times. So a small vibration at the eardrum is turned into a big vibration of this window at the inner ear.

The third part of the human ear, the inner ear, is full of fluid. The vibrating window sets up pressure waves in the fluid. These pressure waves bend special hairs that grow in the inner ear. When these hair cells are bent, they send electricity into the auditory nerve. The auditory nerve sends these electrical signals to the brain, where they are processed – and finally, you have the sensation of hearing!

And that's the long, complicated story of how pressure waves in the air get turned into the sensation of sound.

with the Royal Victorian Eye and Ear Hospital and Melbourne University's Department of Otolaryngology (the study of ear and throat). They joined forces with the Department of Electrical

The Bionic Ear

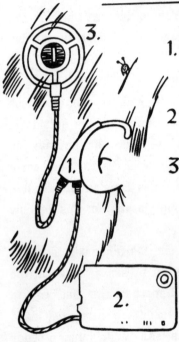

1. Microphone transmits sounds to speech processor.

2. Processor turns sound into electrical signal.

3. Signal sent to transmitting coil which radios signal to receiver/stimulator, buried under the skin. The receiver activates nerves to send sound information to brain.

Engineering, which had the skills that they needed and together they made an artificial ear. Popularly termed the bionic ear, it made them world leaders in the field of hearing aids.

A normal hearing aid just makes sounds louder. It then feeds those sounds into the outer ear, then to the middle and inner ears. You need to have the entire chain of communication intact, from the outer ear to the middle and inner ears, for the hearing aid to be most useful. But if the chain is broken or badly damaged, a hearing aid is useless. Then, you need a bionic ear.

For example, somebody who has had the bones in their inner ear totally destroyed by disease, so that sound energy cannot travel any further than the middle ear, would not benefit from a hearing aid, but they are a suitable candidate for a bionic ear. A bionic ear directly stimulates the auditory nerve in the inner ear, bypassing the chain of communication between the three parts.

The proper name for the bionic ear is 'cochlear implant', because part of it is actually fitted in the inner ear, in the cochlea.

The bionic ear has a number of parts outside the body as well as inside. It works as follows. First of all, a microphone picks up all sounds, including speech. The

Who is Deaf?

On average, about one baby out of every 1000 is born deaf, and about one person per 1000 will become deaf at some stage in their lifetime. In America alone, about 2 million people are profoundly deaf. Of these 2 million people, about one-quarter (500,000) could benefit from a cochlear implant.

A Deaf Father Led to Hearing for Thousands

Graeme Clark's father was a pharmacist. Often he would have difficulty in hearing a customer and he would have to ask them to speak more loudly. Both he and the customer would get embarrassed about the customer's medical problems being loudly proclaimed in a shop full of other customers.

In 1967, Graeme Clark began the research that led to the invention of the bionic ear. For many years, his work was handicapped by lack of funds. But in 1974, Channel 10 in Melbourne staged a Telethon to raise money for his research. With the money, he built a simple bionic ear, and tested it on a deaf man called Rod Saunders. The bionic ear worked, and Rod could hear again!

sound then gets sent to a speech processor, which concentrates on speech and tries to ignore other noise. The speech processor turns sounds into electrical signals which are sent to an FM radio transmitter. The transmitter turns the electrical signals into radio waves. The advantage of having the signals enter the ear as radio waves is that there is no need for wires, which could lead to infection within the ear.

The rest of the bionic ear is implanted into the body. A receiver, which is also a stimulator, is wrapped in silicone rubber — because silicone is usually ignored by the body's immune system. The package fits into a little hole, cut by a surgeon, in the mastoid bone (the one just behind your ear). The receiver picks up the transmitted radio waves and turns them back into electrical signals, which are carried to special electrodes fitted into the cochlea to stimulate the auditory nerve. From there the signals travel down the auditory nerve to the brain. The brain can interpret these signals as sounds.

At first, the bionic ear was tried on adults and, later, on younger and younger children. The latest push is to adapt it for children under two years of age, because they will benefit hugely from it. Almost everybody gets *some* improvement in hearing — and talking — from the bionic ear.

The speech processor has been much improved since the early days. Consider the most difficult test of all — a deaf person trying to listen to speech over the telephone. In this case, they can't use their skill in lip-reading. Back in 1985, deaf adults using an early version of the speech processor understood only 12% of words that were spoken over the phone, but the 1996 speech processor increased this to 78%!

This new version of the bionic ear uses a silicon microchip about the size of a small fingernail. But it has 8000 transistors in it. It is better than previous versions, but still not as good as the human ear.

Super-sensitive Ear

The undamaged ear of a young person is very sensitive. It can turn very small vibrations at the eardrum into perception of sound in the brain — even if the vibrations are as small as one-billionth of a centimetre. That's about one-tenth of the size of a hydrogen atom!

If the human ear were *more* sensitive, you would hear an annoying hiss as air molecules constantly hit your eardrum!

The human ear has some 30,000 hair cells that send signals to the auditory nerve. The current bionic ear has only 22 electrodes to send signals to the auditory nerve.

Professor Graeme Clark's team had successfully finished the first part of their research project, to develop the bionic ear, by 1978. By 1981, they had become part of an Australian company called the Nucleus Group. There are now several companies that make bionic ears, but the Nucleus Group was the first and still enjoys a large share of the world market.

While it is very difficult to repair a damaged ear, it is very easy to protect a good ear from going deaf due to loud sound. Loud noise is dangerous, and it's everywhere — dance parties, kindergartens, and building sites, where you hear power tools like saws and angle grinders.

Try to wear ear protection if you are in a very noisy place. Remember, a thrash concert is as loud as a jumbo 747 at 100 metres, which is as loud as a screaming four-year-old at half a metre!

Floating Metals

Around the turn of the 20th century, a brewer's invention made Australia one of the wealthiest countries on the planet. However, his invention did not make money from beer — it made money from leftover rock! It probably earned more money for Australia than any other single Australian invention. His invention is still the most commonly used method of separating rock from the precious minerals or metals inside them.

Much of Australia's wealth comes from mining. The miners take the rock out of the ground to remove the metals that they want from the rock, These days, they have to meet standards for cleaning up the mining site when they're finished with it.

Mining gives us the metals or minerals that our society needs and, unfortunately, a pile of leftover rocks called 'mine tailings'.

Even today, it's impossible to get all the metals out of the rock. The mine tailings still have some useful metals left in them. Mine tailings can be worth a lot of money.

Broken Hill is one of the most famous silver, lead and zinc mines in the world. After it was discovered in 1883 engineers quickly found ways to remove about half of the silver and two-thirds of the lead from the rock. Practically all of the zinc and the rest of the silver and lead were left behind mixed in with the tailings. (By the early 1900s, 6 million tonnes of zinc alone were locked in the mine tailings at Broken Hill.)

What was thrown away was worth more than all the metal that had been taken out. But when the price of zinc dropped in the late 1890s, the tailings also dropped in value. If they were going to get the zinc out, they would have to do so very cheaply.

In 1903, there were £30 million worth of metals locked into the tailings at Broken Hill. The 20,000 people living in Broken Hill had poverty staring them in the face, because nobody could remove the valuable metals from the tailings at a cheap price. As far as everybody was concerned, the tailings were useless, and Broken Hill might soon be broke! Duncan McBryde, the Chairman of BHP (Broken Hill Proprietary Limited), said that the entire future of the company, and therefore the town, depended on being able to treat the ores. But it was a very

Charles Rasp and His Book

In 1844, the explorer Charles Sturt collected some samples from a strangely coloured hill with a 'broken back' in the western part of New South Wales. However, he had to toss these interesting samples aside during a difficult crossing of a desert further inland.

One year later, in 1845, Charles Rasp was born in Germany. He later became a chemist and came to Australia when he was 23 years old. He soon started working as a boundary rider, checking the fences on a huge property in the western part of New South Wales. He would look out from his accommodation at a small broken hill that his fellow workers had already dismissed as 'just another hill'. One day, he rode out to the hill on his horse. He swung himself to the ground, taking out of his saddle bags a hammer and a book. The book was *Goyder's Mining Guide*. It turned out that the 'broken hill' was actually one of the richest deposits of silver, lead and zinc ever discovered. Within 20 years, he was a millionaire.

hard problem — an American consultant said that it was the most difficult problem ever encountered in the history of metallurgy!

The traditional method used to separate metals from rocks was to melt the rock. Each metal melts at a different temperature. Let's suppose you are gradually heating up the rock. As the temperature rises, first one metal melts. You can pour it off into a container and let it cool down. Then you heat up the rock a bit more, until the second metal melts. You pour that metal into a different container. You keep on doing this to get the metals you want. This method works, but it is very expensive. It takes a lot of costly energy to melt a solid rock into a liquid.

For nearly half a century engineers had been working on another way to separate metal from rock, but they hadn't perfected it yet. It would eventually be called the 'flotation process', because it floats a metal on water. You would think that metal sinks in water, as it is much denser. The trick is that you work with tiny particles of metal, not big blocks. The surface tension of the water will hold tiny particles of metal on the surface, in the same way that it will hold grains of pepper. The problem then is how to lift them off. The answer is bubbles.

The first stage is to smash the rock down to particles about the size of grains of sand. This is fairly cheap and easy to do. One way is to smash it with giant mechanical hammers. In the olden days, these hammers were driven by steam. Another way is to put the rock into a large steel drum, about 2 metres in diameter and 10 metres deep — roughly the size of a large container on the back of a semi-trailer. Into the steel drum, you put pieces of super-hard steel — either long steel bars or thousands of steel balls. Then you rotate the drum. Soon, all the rock has been turned into a coarse powder, like ground pepper or salt. One tiny particle of rock might be rich in lead, while another might be rich in zinc.

The second stage is to add a liquid to the powdered rock. This liquid can be water, or oil or sulphuric acid.

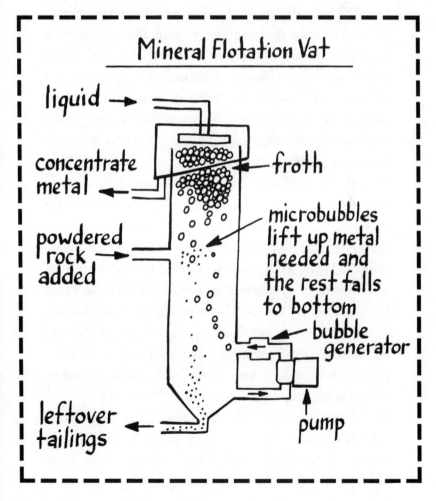

Mineral Flotation Vat

liquid →

concentrate metal ←

← froth

powdered rock added →

microbubbles lift up metal needed and the rest falls to bottom

← bubble generator

leftover tailings ←

pump

In the third stage, you make bubbles at the bottom of the liquid. If you choose the right liquid, the bubbles will rise and lift up only the metal that you want, leaving other metals behind. Then you skim off the frothing bubbles at the surface with a scraper.

At this stage, the froth is very rich in your chosen metal. Then you heat the froth to melt the metal. Because you're melting just a small amount of rock you use much less energy, and this is the great advantage of the flotation process. It is cheaper to melt a small percentage of the rock at any one time than all of it. Many people worked for a long time to develop this idea of using liquids or bubbles to float tiny particles of metal.

In 1860, William Haynes of England put out a patent on a process that used liquids to separate minerals — in his case, sulphur minerals. He pulverised the rock and mixed it with oil. The sulphur minerals stuck to the oil. He washed the mixture with a powerful jet of water. The particles that were stuck to the oil didn't budge. The particles that hadn't stuck to the oil were washed away. This is because oil and water don't mix with each other. It was a washing process, not a true flotation process, but it was a step in the right direction.

In 1877, the Bessel brothers of Dresden, in Germany, had a patent on a flotation process to separate graphite ores. Graphite, a type of carbon, is the 'lead' in pencils. They first pulverised graphite

Why is Beer Froth White?

Beer is a dark liquid and yet the bubbles and the froth at the top of the glass are white. It's the same with cola drinks — they are dark in colour, but the bubble and froth are light-coloured. Why is this so?

The first thing to realise is that each beer bubble is hollow and that the wall of the bubble is made from beer. Because the wall is made from a dark liquid, it stops much of the light from getting into the hollow inside the bubble. So, in each bubble you have a smooth wall with lots of light on one side and not much light on the other side. This is the same as looking at the glass windows of an office in daytime. There is a lot of light on one side of the window glass, and not much on the other side. If you're on the side where there is lots of light, the window glass acts like a mirror and reflects your image.

In the same way, when you're looking at a bubble, you're on the side with a lot of light, so the wall of the bubble is reflecting the light. In other words, each bubble is a tiny mirror! Mirrors just reflect the local light and in most cases the light outside the bubble is white in colour — so that's why the bubbles look white. But if you change the colour of the light (say, by putting red light bulbs in your kitchen), then the colour of the bubbles will change.

ore, and then added oil and water to the powder. The process worked, but it was not well publicised and was lost to history.

The first successful large-scale flotation process was designed by Charles Potter, a brewer of beer.

Brewing has always involved liquids, solid particles and froths. At the brewery, Charles Potter saw the way the beer froth lifted up the sediment in the beer. That's probably where his ideas came from.

Charles Potter came from Melbourne. He was a chemist, a brewer and a bit of an inventor. He had already invented a new stopper for bottles, a better way to make malt and an improved nosebag for feeding horses.

Around 1900, he began to think about the problems of Broken Hill and all that wasted zinc sitting in the tailings. His plan was to add hot sulphuric acid (H_2SO_4) to the zinc-filled tailings. The acid would react with the zinc and release little bubbles of the gas carbon dioxide. Bubbles of carbon dioxide would then stick to the zinc particles and carry them up to the surface of the acid. Once the zinc was floating at the top of the acid bath, it was easily skimmed off! The rest of the waste rock stayed at the bottom.

In 1901 Potter took out a patent on his work. By 1903, he had built a small plant in Broken Hill which could recover 60% of the zinc available in the ore.

But somebody else had a very similar idea. Guillaume Delprat had originally trained in physics, but had later turned to engineering and then mining. He became General Manager of BHP at Broken Hill.

Delprat used Potter's basic idea, but he didn't use sulphuric acid. Instead he used saltcake (its chemical

Charles Potter discovers mineral flotation

name is $NaHSO_4$). The saltcake had the same effect as the sulphuric acid — the zinc stuck to the bubbles that formed and then floated to the top.

Potter felt that Delprat had stolen his idea. He sued Delprat, which meant he was suing BHP, a giant company. The court case went on for four years. BHP said that Potter's design wasn't a good design. BHP claimed that while sulphuric acid did work, it didn't work as well as saltcake. BHP won the court case. But then BHP went ahead and used Potter's sulphuric acid idea anyway! It seems that Potter's design wasn't as useless as the court had been led to believe.

Today, the process is called the Potter–Delprat Process. At least Potter got his name first!

In 1905, it was found that air bubbles worked just as well as bubbles of carbon dioxide. The air bubbles were cheap and easy to make, by simply stirring up water with a big paddle.

Although by 1912 nearly all zinc sulphide ores could be separated from the waste rock by using the bubbles of the mineral flotation process, there was still a problem — particles of galena (lead sulphide) were often mixed in with the zinc sulphide floating on the surface.

In 1912, a carpenter by the name of James Lyster was working with the Zinc Corporation. He invented a flotation process that separated the lead and zinc.

Sewage and Bubbles

Sewage systems to take away toilet wastes have been found in the ruins of prehistoric cities in Crete. Back then, with a low population, they would channel the toilet wastes into the ocean without causing too much pollution. But with today's much higher populations, we just can't keep doing this. One popular way of processing sewage to get rid of the solid wastes uses flotation. They just bubble air through the sewage while it sits in tanks. Up to 75% of the solid wastes bubble to the surface, where they are skimmed off. They are either taken out to sea and dumped or buried inland — still not very satisfactory ways of disposal.

Lyster discovered that when he used an alkaline solution, the lead floated and the zinc did not. But the alkaline solution had to be hot. His process worked, but it used lots of expensive energy for heating. Then he discovered that if he added eucalyptus oil the solution didn't have to be heated. He needed only 200 grams of eucalyptus oil per tonne of crushed rock to make the process work!

Today many different chemicals are used to float the minerals from crushed rock, a result of Lyster's experimentation.

The basic idea, however, remains unchanged. Suppose you have a rock with a complex mix of metals such as copper, lead, iron and zinc. The flotation process has made it economically worthwhile to process that rock.

Broken Hill had 'floated' 8 million tonnes of rock by 1911 and was producing one-fifth of all the world's zinc. This practical knowledge spread from Broken Hill to the rest of the world.

Mineral flotation was worth big money to companies all over the world. In 1942 alone, America treated 140 million tonnes of crushed rock! These days, Australia is the world's second largest exporter of zinc. Zinc is used everywhere — for galvanising, car bodies, batteries, cosmetics, paints, inks and in the coating of television sets. Australia produces about 11% of the world's lead. Lead is used in car batteries, solder and radiation shielding.

Other Inventors of Froth Flotation

It often happens in the fields of science and technology that many people come up with the same idea around the same time. In 1898, H.F.K. Picard and Henry Livingstone Sulman began a partnership as metallurgical consultants in London. After some years, they came up with a bubble flotation process.

Two other British technologists also came up the idea of flotation, roughly around the same time. They were brothers – Francis Edward Elmore and Alexander Stanley Elmore. In 1898, Francis patented a process called the 'bulk oil process'. This process used an oil, not bubbles, to float small particles of ground rock to the surface of a liquid. It took a lot of trial and error to get the flotation process to work. Worldwide, some 50 people in 11 different companies worked on the flotation process between 1902 and 1915.

In the 1980s, Professor Graeme Jameson and his students at the University of Newcastle invented an improved flotation process. It's cheaper than the old process, because there are no motors or moving parts. And the bubbles and the particles of rock can mix better, so more of the metal you want comes to the surface. The Jameson Cell Ore Process is now being used around the world.

(Of course, lead has to be handled very carefully, and it is especially dangerous to children.)

Many soft drinks have lots of bubbles. Now, I wonder what would happen if you mixed them up in a vat with mine tailings ...

Copper Flotation

Copper has been used by humans for 7000 years. In the early days, people would find lumps of almost pure copper just lying on the ground, but those days are long gone. Today, about 80% of all copper comes from rocks that contain less than 2% copper by weight.

This copper ore is crushed into a fine powder and mixed with water and other chemicals. One of these chemicals acts on the copper to make it 'dislike' water. To 'get away' from the water, the copper sticks to the bubbles of air and gets carried to the surface. The bubbles are skimmed off with a blade and then heated to about 800°C. This removes the water, as well as a few unwanted minerals such as arsenic, antimony and sulphur. The stuff left behind is mixed with silica and then heated further to about 1450°C. More processing brings the copper to about 98% purity. The copper is refined to over 99.95% purity with electrolytic refining.

Forests, Fleece & Prickly Pears

Contents

Prickly Pear

Until the early 20th century one of the worst threats to Australian agriculture was a rather pretty cactus called the 'prickly pear'. Australia barely won the battle against the imported prickly pear cactus.

'Prickly pear' is a term used to cover all members of the genus *Opuntia*, but in New South Wales the term is extended to include all members of the cactus family. Cactus species, with the exception of one species, all originate from North and South America and neighbouring islands.

At the moment, there are some 35 different species of cactus that have taken root in Australia. Only three have become major pests. The most important of these were two varieties of *Opuntia stricta*, *Opuntia stricta* variety *stricta* (previously referred to as *Opuntia inermis*) and *Opuntia stricta* variety *dillenii*. The other two species that were problems in the past were *Opuntia aurantiaca* and *Harrisia martinii*. All species are now controlled by insect biological control agents.

The first species of prickly pear that was brought out to Australia was *Opuntia vulgaris*. It arrived very early, with the First Fleet in 1788. This prickly pear was picked up in Rio de Janeiro. The First Fleeters wanted to be able to make their own red dye, so they carried with them some prickly pear plants and some cochineal insects, *Dactylopius ceylonicus*. They planned to feed cochineal insects with prickly pear. The insects would then be ground up to make a red dye. (Even today, red food colouring is called cochineal.)

This first introduced species of prickly pear caused problems in coastal areas, although it probably didn't become well established from this first introduction. (It didn't start up a pink dye industry, either.)

But as the years rolled by people brought more species of prickly pear into Australia. They brought

Chemical Control

Often chemicals are the only way that we have of controlling pests and making sure that we have a food crop.

But chemicals have their disadvantages. They have to be used again and again, as the chemicals deteriorate and the pests come back. Some of these chemicals can also be very expensive.

Often the pests will develop a resistance to the chemicals, so new chemicals have to be brought into play.

And unfortunately chemicals can sometimes kill friendly and useful plants and insects.

them in for animal feed, for hedges, or just as something pretty to look at. People didn't realise just how efficient these cacti were at spreading across the land. Like other plants, most cacti spread by seed. But they had another trick up their sleeve — they could also grow from segments that look like leaves. If these segments come into contact with the ground they put down roots and grow into new plants.

It seems that *Opuntia stricta* variety *stricta*, common prickly pear (one of the nasty ones), was brought to Scone around 1839. Almost immediately, neighbours took cuttings from it, and so it began to spread. In 1843, somebody took it to Yandilla in Queensland.

This cactus loved the relatively hot, dry climate in New South Wales and Queensland. It grew like

Biological Control – Bad

An important crop in Queensland is sugar cane. Unfortunately the larvae of the grey-back beetle damage sugar cane. So in 1935, the cane toad was imported from Hawaii to Queensland to eat the grey-back beetle. It was released without any testing – this type of release is not permitted today.

It was a disaster. The cane toad did not seem to be interested in the grey-back beetle. It preferred to eat native bees and other useful insects instead. Today the cane toad is a real pest.

crazy. Soon whole paddocks were covered with the cactus. Much of the land became useless for farming or grazing animals.

In 1883, the Queensland Government realised how bad prickly pear was and started urging farmers to get rid of it. They officially called it a 'noxious weed'. By 1884, the Brisbane *Courier* expressed the feelings of the general public when it asked for *some means whereby the growing evil can be overcome.*

But how were they going to get rid of the cactus? There was so much of it to remove. Ripping it out by hand, or poisoning it, just created a small area free of cactus — which the cactus overran again almost immediately!

By 1900, about 4 million hectares (40,000 square

kilometres) of land were covered by prickly pear. The areas most affected were between Mackay in Queensland and the Hunter Valley in New South Wales, a distance of about 1500 km. About 85% of the infestation was in Queensland and 15% in New South Wales.

A long drought ended in 1902 and the rains encouraged the prickly pear to grow even more. Soon prickly pear was covering land at about half a million hectares per year!

By 1912 the Queensland Government realised that the situation was well and truly out of control, so it set up the Prickly Pear Travelling Commission. The Commission sent two scientists overseas to countries where prickly pear was native and to countries where it had been introduced. The Commission looked for natural enemies of the prickly pear.

The scientists sent a cochineal insect, *Dactylopius ceylonicus*, back to Australia. This insect was then introduced into parts of Queensland. This cochineal was collected from *Opuntia vulgaris* (which had come with the First Fleet) and caused a lot of damage to this cactus in Queensland. Unfortunately, this cochineal insect just wasn't interested in *Opuntia stricta*.

The Prickly Pear Travelling Commission set up a field station at Chinchilla, a town in central Queensland on the Warrego Highway. It started

Biological Control – Good

Biological control means getting one living creature to control another living creature – for the good of the human race!

For example, if we have trouble with a weed and we want to get rid of it, we could poison it with chemicals – although that might also kill useful plants.

But if we could get an insect that would eat that weed, then we could release that insect near the weed. Of course, we would first have to make sure that the insect would not eat other plants, or bring diseases (virus, bacteria, fungus etc.) into our country, or have any other bad effects. It would be nice if, when the weed had all gone, the insect would also die out.

The first known example of biological control was in 1888. An Australian insect, the cottony-cushion scale, had somehow set up home in California, and it was eating the citrus plants, such as oranges and lemons. The Californian citrus growers couldn't stop it. Then somebody realised that another Australian insect, the ladybird, loved to eat the scale. The ladybird was imported and had rid California of most of the scale insect within two years.

This first example of biological control was an amazing success. The ladybird was then exported to another 50 countries around the world, with similarly spectacular results.

experimenting with ways to poison prickly pears. At the same time, biologists looked at many of the different species of prickly pear in Australia. They found at least 11 different species here. But the species causing the biggest problems were two varieties of *Opuntia stricta*.

The prickly pear problem was too big for Queensland to handle by itself, so it combined with the New South Wales and Commonwealth Governments to form the Commonwealth Prickly Pear Board in 1920. The Board decided it would use biological control, but it needed more knowledge.

The Board set up a huge international research study to find all the insects that attacked prickly pear. They found 150 potential killers of various cactus species. They brought 50 of these insects back to Australia. These 50 species were tested on many different plants to make sure that after they had eaten prickly pear, they would not start eating

Insects

Insects are the most common life form on the planet; well over 75% of all animals are insects.

There are over 1 million different species of insects in the world. Practically all of these species do good for humans, or at least don't bother us.

Fewer than 10,000 species of insects cause any harm to the human race.

useful plants. After thorough testing, the Board released 12 of these insects.

But while all this research was going on, prickly pear kept spreading. By the 1920s, prickly pear had covered 20 million hectares (200,000 square kilometres) of land and had made it useless for farming. The cactus was now spreading at the rate of one million hectares a year (roughly 2 hectares a minute!). The worst year was probably 1925, when 26 million hectares (260,000 square kilometres) were covered by prickly pear. Australia has a total surface area of about 7,682,300 square kilometres, so prickly pear had covered about 3.4% of that area. This is enormous, especially when you consider that less than 10% of Australia's land is considered really suitable for growing of crops.

The prickly pear gladiator!

The only hope for Australian agriculture was that at least one of these imported insects would cause significant damage to prickly pear. We were lucky. Alan P. Dodd, the scientist in charge of the investigation at that

Prickly Pear – Good

Even though prickly pears caused enormous destruction in Australia, some people found uses for it.

Apparently, the fruit of the prickly pear is delicious. The skin and its small thorns (glochids) are usually peeled off before eating. People used to make jam out of the fruit. However, the black prickly pear seeds are hard to digest. So after eating prickly pear jam (with the seeds still in it) you can end up very constipated!

Farmers also used the fruit of the prickly pear to feed their cows.

The spikes of the cactus were used as needles to play records (those old-fashioned flat, round, black vinyl things that people had before CDs and MP3 players were invented.)

time, was rather impressed by a moth, *Cactoblastis cactorum*, from northern Argentina and southern Brazil.

This moth lays its eggs in a long chain (or 'stick') of 75 to 80 eggs somewhere on the cactus. A few weeks later, the caterpillars hatch out. The baby caterpillars chomp right into the cactus near the base of the egg stick. They eat their way into the soft flesh and hollow out the inside of each segment and the remainder usually rots. If caterpillar numbers are high enough, many plants die.

Alan P. Dodd sent just one shipment of *Cactoblastis cactorum* to Australia — but it was enough. That consignment of 3000 eggs reached the quarantine station in Sherwood, a suburb of Brisbane, in May 1925. The eggs hatched into caterpillars — and what they loved to eat best of all was the two nasty varieties of prickly pear!

The caterpillars turned into cocoons, and then into moths. In September 1925, the next generation of moths laid 100,000 eggs. The whole cycle started again, egg–caterpillar–cocoon–moth, and by March 1926 there were 2.5 million eggs!

By the end of 1927, 9 million eggs had been released. The effects began to be seen in June 1928, when these eggs had hatched into living caterpillars and started eating and killing hundreds of hectares of prickly pear. By March 1929, 300 million eggs had been distributed from the Sherwood quarantine station, and the moth became established over huge areas.

As the moths rapidly increased, prickly pear began to suffer. By 1930, there was a sudden decline of the prickly pear, and many of the

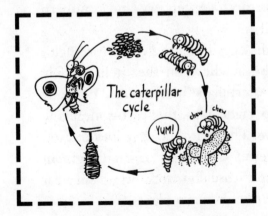

The caterpillar cycle

chew chew

YUM!

moths, with nothing else to eat, also died. So there was a sudden increase in the prickly pear from 1931 to 1933 — but the moth numbers soon increased again, once there was food to eat.

By 1933, only seven years after the moths' release, most of the prickly pear in Australia was rotting on the ground. Alan P. Dodd was so impressed with the moth that he wrote: *The conquest of the prickly pear has been due almost entirely to this remarkable insect. Its introduction brought about a complete change in the outlook within a few years. Its progress has been spectacular; its achievements border on the miraculous. Great tracts of country, utterly useless on account of the dense growth of the weed, have been brought into production. The prickly pear territory has been transformed as though by magic from a wilderness to a scene of prosperous endeavour.*

The people of the Queensland dairy farming area of Boonarga (near Chinchilla) were so pleased with the moth's progress that they erected the Cactoblastis Memorial Hall in its honour. In 1995, Wendy McCarthy, the Chair of the Australian Heritage Commission, said: 'The Boonarga Cactoblastis Memorial Hall is believed to be the only hall in the world erected to the memory of an insect.'

Even today the prickly pear is not completely wiped out, however. The Prickly Pear Destruction Commission in New South Wales ceased to exist in 1987, but cactus species were still covered under a separate Act, the *Prickly Pear Act*, until 1997. In 1997 prickly pears were transferred to the *Noxious Weeds Act*. Cactoblastis needs to go through two generations per year to control common prickly pear. Where this does not occur, another species of cochineal insect, *Dactylopius puntiae*, is used to kill plants.

Thanks to friendly insects, we have controlled the prickly pear in Australia.

Merino Breeding and the Death Penalty

Today Australia has about 15% of all the sheep in the world, but it supplies 30% of *all* wool sold, and 70% of all wool sold to make clothing. It all happened because of a strange animal called the merino sheep, which was stolen from Spain. Merinos now make up about 75% of all sheep in Australia. But there's not just one kind of merino — there are over 200 different types!

We humans have bred sheep for over 9000 years. The result of breeding was that sheep evolved to have the qualities that we wanted — such as lots of wool, lots of meat, the ability to withstand different climates and so on. Sheep have two coats — a protective, outer coat made of long, coarse hairs, and a softer, inner coat made from shorter, soft, fine hairs. Some sheep were bred to have more of the fleecy inner coat and less of the coarser outer coat.

The Romans wrote that the Spaniards had some small sheep with a fine coat; we know that the merino sheep was still in Spain by the 12th century. Over the next few centuries, the Spaniards continued to breed the merino to get a top-quality wool.

By the 1700s, the merino sheep of Spain had the best wool in the known world. The Spanish were making lots of money from their high-quality merino wool.

At first, to keep a monopoly, the Spanish king would not let any merino sheep leave the country. He even imposed the death penalty on people trying to smuggle out his beloved merinos. This meant no one else could breed merinos, and the only place to buy this fine wool was Spain.

But politics is complicated, and sometimes the King had to give merinos to other royal houses in

Europe. In 1723, for instance, a few merinos went to Sweden. The climate didn't really suit them, so they didn't flourish. In 1765, the Spanish king allowed some 92 merino rams and 128 merino ewes to be sent to Saxony in Germany. In 1786, Louis XVI of France also managed to get a few hundred merino sheep. Over the following years, the French bred these merinos with their Rambouillet sheep. Today, the Rambouillet is the largest sheep that gives a fine quality wool.

The English also wanted some of these magnificent sheep. George III was King of England from 1760 to 1820. He was actually quite a keen farmer himself. (His nickname was 'Farmer George' — an odd nickname for a king!) He owned a farm at Kew, and he desperately wanted some of

Longest Fleece

In November 1990, a merino sheep was shorn after seven years of continuous wool growth. This animal was from Willow Springs Station in South Australia. The fleece was 63.5 cm long, and weighed 29.48 km – a record, according to the 1993 *Guinness Book of Records.*

In September 1986, Dr C.A. van der Merwe from South Africa said: 'The merino is the only sheep in the world that can produce 10 to 15% of its live mass in clean wool.'

Oldest Tamed Animals

According to the 1993 *Guinness Book of Records*, the first known animals that were successfully tamed were goats, in Iran, around 7700 BC. In Greece, excavations show that sheep were domesticated by 7200 BC, while domestic cattle and pigs were being bred by 7000 BC. Chickens were tamed in Indochina around 6000 BC.

the fine Spanish merinos, but nobody would give him any.

By chance, on an ocean voyage an English fleet met with a Spanish fleet. Each admiral of the fleet swapped gifts as a gesture of goodwill. The Spaniards gave the British crew some live sheep.

The Spaniards thought the sheep would be killed and eaten — fresh meat was a real rarity on an ocean voyage in those days. This was long before the invention days of refrigeration. But the cunning English kept the sheep alive.

When the fleet arrived back in England, Sir Joseph Banks happened to see the sheep. (Sir Joseph Banks was the botanist who accompanied Captain Cook on his voyages.) He recognised the sheep as the precious Spanish merinos that George III wanted. He immediately made the crew 'give' the sheep to the King.

But unfortunately, all the sheep were ewes —

not one was a ram. Back then it was impossible to produce more sheep when they were all of the same sex!

The King had had no luck when he asked the Spanish Ambassador in London, so he knew it wasn't possible to get the rams legally from the Spaniards. So, he asked his advisors to work out a scheme. Now, the Spaniards have always had a reputation for being a nation of horse-lovers, and at a previous opening of the English Parliament a pair of cream-coloured horses had pulled the Royal Carriage. George's advisors remembered how excited the Spanish Ambassador's wife had been about these magnificent horses.

They decided to try to arrange a deal, involving these horses, with the Ambassador's wife. But there were no other cream-coloured horses in all of England — George III had the only two! Finally, the advisors got a pair of cream horses from overseas at

Good Wool

If your cotton T-shirt gets wet, the water passes through onto your skin, making you cold and wet.

When wool gets wet, it keeps hold of, or hangs onto, the water. It can carry up to 18% of its weight in water. Gradually, your body heat warms up the water and the wet wool acts as an insulating layer.

the huge cost of £8000. They offered them to the señora in exchange for a few Spanish merino rams.

She really wanted the horses, and was prepared to take the risk of being condemned to death. She hired smugglers to steal some rams and get them out of Spain. The smugglers took the rams over the Pyrenees and delivered them to a ship in Hamburg. The English then shipped the sheep to England for the King's flock!

Sheep Gave Us Weights

In the old days before the metric system, we had the Imperial System of measurement in Australia. The Imperial System came from England.

In the Imperial System, one weight measurement was called a 'stone' (about 6.35 kg), but before the Imperial System was devised, a 'stone' was just any decent-sized stone that the people in a village would decide to use as a 'standard' weight. Of course, a stone would have different weights in different villages.

In the 1300s, England began to export raw wool to Florence and it became essential to have a fixed standard of weight. So in 1389, a 'stone' of wool was defined to be 14 pounds (a pound is about 454 grams). In America, which does not use the metric system, the stone is still used as a weight measurement for people and animals.

The first sheep in Australia were brought over with the First Fleet — some Cape Fat Tail sheep. These sheep had fairly hairy tails and a coarse coat, so they were more suited for breeding for meat, not wool. These sheep didn't like eating the coarse grasses that grew on the Australian coast and didn't really thrive.

In 1793, John Macarthur, a Captain in the New South Wales Army Corps, imported some 60 Bengal lambs and ewes to Sydney. Later he bought two

Irish ewes and a ram. When he crossed the Bengal and Irish sheep, he saw that the new baby lambs had a coat that was a curiously mixed fleece of hair and wool. Then, four years later, he had an opportunity to get hold of some merinos.

In 1797, two ships, HMS *Supply* and HMS *Reliance* sailed into Table Bay (the port at the Cape of Good Hope, on the southern tip of South Africa). They had come from England, and had dropped in to pick up food for the new colony in New South Wales.

Some years previously, the Spanish King had presented a collection of merino sheep to the Dutch Royal House. These very special merinos came directly from the Spanish royal flock. They had very thick fleeces of a very fine wool. The merinos had not done well in the damp climate of Holland. In 1789, the Dutch Government gave four Spanish merino ewes and two Spanish merino rams to Colonel Jacob Gordon, the Governor at the Cape.

Expensive Sheep

According to the 1993 *Guinness Book of Records*, the most expensive sheep was one that was sold for $450,000! This animal came from the Collinsville stud, and was sold at the 1989 Adelaide Ram Sales.

Expensive Wool

According to the 1993 *Guinness Book of Records*, the most expensive bale of wool was a super-fine fleece that sold in Tasmania on 23 February 1989, for $3008.50 per kilogram!

They thrived in the drier climate of South Africa.

After these two ships had moored in Table Bay, their Captains (Kent and Waterhouse) were approached by Mrs Gordon, the widow of Colonel Gordon. She wanted to sell the merinos. Unfortunately, the Commissary of the Colony of New South Wales, who was a passenger, refused to make the decision to buy the merinos by himself.

Luckily, the two captains each decided to buy 13 sheep, with the hope of selling them in New South Wales and making a profit. Thirteen was a lucky number that day!

Most of the sheep on the HMS *Supply* died on the long journey to Sydney, but most of the sheep on the HMS *Reliance* survived. Captain Waterhouse sold the surviving sheep to various landholders and New South Wales Corps officers, including the Reverend Samuel Marsden, William Cox, John Rowley, and a certain Captain John Macarthur.

John Macarthur bought four rams and two ewes to start his flock. In 1805, Macarthur imported a further five merino rams and one ewe. He raised his sheep on some land called Cowpastures (now known as Camden) southwest of Sydney. John Macarthur got his name in the history books as the 'Father of the Wool Industry in Australia'. But he actually spent most of his time overseas, living the high life. It was his wife, Elizabeth Macarthur, who was largely responsible for their success in raising sheep — but she hasn't usually been given the credit she deserves. In fact,

The George Peppin merino...

Useful Sheep

Sheep give us wool to cover ourselves with. They also give us milk and meat. The meat of a young sheep is called lamb, while the meat of an older sheep is called mutton.

she was probably the most successful of the early sheep breeders.

People like the Macarthurs and Samuel Marsden got the merino breed started in Australia, but it was the Peppin family that really established the breed. Without George Peppin, Australia would not have the huge merino flocks that it has today.

George Peppin saw that a bigger, bulky-fleeced merino was needed for the dry areas of Queensland and New South Wales. He thought it was more important to have a merino that would survive bad seasons than one that would give lots of fine wool in a good season, but die in a bad season. So, beginning in 1861, Peppin bred together all the different types of merinos he could find across the world — from the royal flocks of George IV in England, from Saxony in Germany, the Cape of Good Hope in South Africa, Rambouillet in France and Vermont in America. These merinos all had different characteristics — for example, the Rambouillet merinos had a fairly coarse wool, but were very robust. He kept picking the largest and bulkiest rams and ewes and mating them with each other.

Charles Massey, the author of *The Australian Merino*, called George Peppin 'The Michelangelo of the Bush': *The Peppin merino may be judged to be Australia's greatest contribution to its own, and the world's, economic and textile development … No other artist works with hidden tools, as the sheep breeder must do when*

Australian Sheep – Good & Bad

For many years, Australian sheep products, such as wool and meat, have been sold overseas. Sheep have given Australia much of its income – which is good.

But as the flocks of sheep got bigger in the 1800s, more land was needed. Sheep numbers went from 250,000 in the mid-1820s, to 1 million in 1830, and 5 million in 1840. So, huge areas of Australia were taken away from the Aborigines. As the flocks moved in, they changed the local ecology. For one thing, they loved to eat the vegetable that was a staple of the Aboriginal diet, the yam.

In fact, the Peppin sheep were really bad for the environment, because they could survive in rough countryside that was drought-stricken. Not only do they pull the grass right out of the soil by its roots, but they also cut the soil with their cloven hooves, so that it can blow away in a dry wind.

handling genetics … No other artist works for four or more decades on a single masterpiece, while contending with a whole range of natural, and sometimes human, forces arrayed against him. And no other artist has a masterpiece as intangible and fluid as the gene pool that constitutes a stud flock.

By the time he died in 1872, George Peppin had bred sheep that gave up to three-quarters of a kilogram more wool than other merinos. They also provided good meat, and were better at surviving droughts.

He tried to make the sheep hardier and, at the same time, have a bigger fleece. He succeeded. In 1800, the average merino fleece weighed less than 2 kg. Today, most ewes at the bigger studs in Australia will give more than 7 kg of wool.

His sheep were superior, but it took a while for conservative farmers to see the benefits of the Peppin sheep. His sons, George and Frederick, carried on his good work. It was certainly appreciated by the South African sheep breeders, who imported large numbers of Peppin sheep to improve their local merinos.

Today, nearly 60% of the sheep in Australia have Peppin blood in them. This is clear and simple proof of the value of his work!

Rabbit

In Australia we've had quite a few rabbit plagues.

The cute, little furry bunnies arrived here with the convicts on the First Fleet in 1788. But these bunnies didn't get really well established until 1859, when a man called Thomas Austin set the scene for Australia's first rabbit plague.

Austin lived near Geelong, in Victoria. He must have been a man of habit. Previously, when he lived in England, he always went shooting live animals on the weekends. He wanted to keep up this ritual in Australia. So he got his brother in England to send him out 24 grey rabbits and five hares.

Austin's rabbits multiplied at a great rate, because in their new habitat they had heaps of food and no natural enemies.

Thomas Austin certainly got his shooting practice. He even had the numbers of rabbits he killed recorded monthly in Victorian newspapers. In 1867, he killed 14,263 rabbits on his property! We can only hope that he enjoyed his weekends, because not much else good came from his breeding of rabbits.

The rabbits didn't just run wild on Thomas Austin's property. He was a generous man — he very kindly sent pairs of rabbits to friends around Australia.

By 1867 rabbits had spread throughout most of Victoria. By 1885, over 8000 square kilometres of Victorian farmland had been stripped bare by rabbits and abandoned by settlers. Within 20 years, the rabbits had spread to New South Wales and Queensland. Eventually, rabbits got to every part of Australia, except the really dry deserts and the tropics. In all, they ravaged over 4 million square kilometres of Australia. The only part of Australia where there are hardly any rabbits is north of the Tropic of Capricorn, which crosses Australia near Rockhampton, Alice Springs and Exmouth.

The rabbits forged across Australia, eating every blade of grass and stripping every bush they could reach. They turned some of Australia's green areas into deserts. We have reports from some of the early explorers and surveyors; land they described as green is now desert — even after good rainfalls. Also, by eating and destroying the natural greenery, the

rabbits took away the food of many native animals. Over 60% of the wallaby breeds that used to be in central Australia are now extinct and another 25% are rare or endangered. In other areas, 75% of the native rodents are now extinct.

Around the beginning of the 20th century, thousands of kilometres of fences were built to stop the rabbit invasion. The longest one, in Western Australia, some 1833 km long, was finished in 1907. It ran from Starvation Boat Harbour in the south to Cape Keraudren in the north.

But there was no way that the fences could ever keep out the bunnies. The fences were continually damaged by storms, wombats, kangaroos and emus. They were covered by drifting sand. But the most important reason was that it took so long to build the fences that the bunnies had already reached the other side by the time they were finished!

In 1919, Dr Arago, a Brazilian scientist who studied viruses, realised how big Australia's rabbit problem was. He knew of a virus called myxoma which infected rabbits and gave them a disease called myxomatosis. He told the Australian Government that myxomatosis might be a good weapon against the rabbits. But the government of the day didn't realise how much damage the rabbits were doing, so they turned down his offer. Dr Arago got an official reply, which read: *The trade in rabbits, both fresh and frozen, either for local food or for export, has grown to be one of great importance, and popular sentiment here is opposed to the extermination of the rabbit by the use of some virulent organism.*

In other words, the government didn't want advice on how to kill rabbits, because they thought there was lots of money in rabbits. Years later, they were to eat their words!

Myxoma is a virus that belongs to the same family as smallpox and chickenpox. It can't be spread to people from animals. European rabbits are very susceptible to the myxoma virus. In fact, 90% of them die from their first contact with the virus. But not all rabbits have such a drastic reaction to the

Rabbits and $ – 1

It's hard to get the exact figures on how the bunnies affect our economy.

One popular figure is that the 300 million rabbits cost the Australian economy about $300 million each year in lost agricultural production and damage to the environment. But on the other hand our rabbit industry generates about $20 million to 50 million each year. In some years, as many as 100 million wild rabbits have been killed and exported as meat and fur.

But that still means that the bunnies cost us over $250 million each year.

virus. The American rabbit only gets little skin lumps when it has myxomatosis.

The myxoma virus is spread from one rabbit to the next by insects, such as fleas or mosquitoes. The insect jabs the rabbit with its pointy bit (the proboscis) to have a tiny drink of blood. As the blood flows into the insect, so does some of the virus. The insect then carries the virus to the next rabbit that it bites and that rabbit gets infected — that's why the CSIR (now CSIRO) scientists sometimes gave the insects the nickname of 'flying pins'.

You can see a possible problem here. If there are no fleas or mosquitoes around, a sick rabbit can't

Rabbits and $ – 2

By early 1997, some 29 companies that dealt in rabbits had their business drop almost to nothing as the Calicivirus killed millions of rabbits across Australia. They reckon that they are being driven out of business because the Australian Government accidentally released the Calicivirus before the rabbit industry was ready for it (see pages 150 to 152).

As a result, there are some 29 claims from rabbit sellers for Loss of Income before the Australian Government. The companies claim that their combined annual turnover is about $50 million. They want to be compensated for their loss of income until the year 2010.

spread the disease to a perfectly healthy rabbit right next to it.

Around 1926, the New South Wales Department of Agriculture infected rabbits in the field with myxomatosis, but only a few of the rabbits died. The tests were a flop, because the virus didn't spread into the rabbit population. Back in 1926, they didn't know that the virus had to be carried by an insect from one rabbit to another. In 1934, Dame Jean MacNamara also called for the myxoma virus to be used against the rabbit. She was an expert on poliomyelitis. This is a virus that can cripple and sometimes kill people. While overseas, she sent myxoma virus to Australia for testing on cattle and sheep — but Quarantine destroyed it in case it was a danger to those animals.

Over the next two years, the rabbit plague became worse. So, in 1936, Dr Lionel Bull, a government scientist, gave the all-clear for the CSIR to release the myxoma virus in Australia. Of course, he had first made sure that it wouldn't infect our native animals or our farm animals.

First, CSIR scientists did some tests in a dry part of South Australia. They injected rabbits with the myxoma virus. Then they put the rabbits, sick with myxomatosis, back in their burrows. Again, much to everyone's disappointment, myxomatosis didn't spread easily from one rabbit to the next. At most it would wipe out one burrow. The farmers were not happy. A handful of dead rabbits just wasn't enough. Bull wrote a report saying he didn't think myxomatosis would ever control the rabbit plague in Australia.

By the 1940s, rabbits were almost shoulder to shoulder on the ground. The weather had been exactly right for the bunnies to breed like crazy. By now, World War II was happening, so most of the male farmers were overseas fighting. The women were

Rabbit Families

Rabbits love to hang around in groups. In the breeding season they form little groups of one to three males and one to seven females. There are two bosses, one male and one female. These groups get together when their breeding season starts.

They can start having babies when they are three or four months old and their pregnancy lasts about one month. The babies are born blind and without any fur. But the mother pulls fur from her own legs and tummy and uses it to cover the babies. In her first pregnancy, the mother will have about three or four babies, but this will rise to six or seven by the end of the season.

The more lush the area, the more babies the rabbits can have in one year. This varies from 11 in dry areas to over 25 in southern inland New South Wales.

managing the farms by themselves. Even if the men and women had both been on the farms, they would not have been able to kill the rabbits fast enough.

Sheep and cattle had to compete with the rabbits for food. One hundred rabbits eat as much greenery as one head of cattle. Farms were able to carry only about half their usual number of sheep, because the rabbits had stripped bare all the grazing land. The soil erosion was terrible.

Australia had hundreds of millions of rabbits. Every rabbit cost the economy $1 per year in lost income. Many farmers went bankrupt. The situation was desperate.

By 1949, the rabbits were totally out of control. Dame Jean again lobbied for the use of myxomatosis. Because it was their only hope, the CSIRO, as they were now called, decided to try myxomatosis a second time. Francis Ratcliffe, the head of the Wildlife Survey Section, was in charge of this new project.

They released myxomatosis into the rabbits, just like they had the last time. But this time it happened to be raining.

For the first few weeks, the farmers and the researchers spotted only a few sick rabbits. The researchers got very depressed. It was raining so much that they decided to go back to Canberra to

Rabbit Shooters

The countryside around where New South Wales, South Australia and Queensland meet is called 'the best rabbit country in the world'. Sharpshooters would work for weeks at a time, without a break. They would earn up to $400 for a night's shooting (the rabbits were worth 80 cents each).

These shooters would fire so many bullets that they did not talk of their job in terms of the number of bullets that they fired. Instead, they talked of how many rifle barrels they wore out!

Hot Cross Bunnies

The Box Hill sheep station was, like all other sheep stations, infested with rabbits. At Box Hill, the bunnies had actually built a huge warren under the station's workshop, with hundreds of bunnies living inside.

When lightning hit the workshop one day it burst into flames. The bunnies living underneath the workshop fled from the blaze, but some had their fur catch on fire in the process. As they ran, they started a grass fire which spread over a square kilometre of grazing land and destroyed several buildings.

write their report. They thought they had another myxomatosis failure on their hands.

But one single long-distance phone call changed everything for the scientists. A farmer rang to report that there were sick rabbits everywhere on his property. Every day more reports like this came flooding into the office. Sick rabbits were being spotted up to 1600 km away from where the first rabbits had been infected. The farmers were ecstatic.

The big question now was — why had the myxomatosis spread so well this time, when it had not done so before? The answer lay in the rain. More rain meant more breeding sites for the mosquitoes. More mosquitoes could carry more virus and more rabbits got infected!

Myxomatosis killed up to 80% of the rabbits throughout most of Australia. Grazing land soon recovered. Sheep and cattle once again had enough food. In fact, the value of meat and wool produced increased by $68 million in 1952 and 1953, just two years after myxomatosis was reintroduced.

The myxoma virus was the first real weapon that we had against the bunnies. Unfortunately, it's not as effective now as it was back in the 1950s. For one thing, the virus is getting weaker.

Another reason is that the bunnies are now 'tougher'. In the early days, most of the rabbits that were infected with the myxoma virus died. But some 'tough' rabbits that had a natural slight resistance to the myxoma virus survived. They bred with other 'tough' rabbits and gave birth to babies that also had a resistance to the myxoma virus. Gradually, more and more rabbits developed a resistance to the myxoma virus. Now only about 25% of the bunnies die once they get infected.

In 1968, the CSIRO released another weapon against the bunnies. The myxoma virus could not jump from one bunny to the next unless there were suitable insects. There were lots of insects around when it was wet — but much of Australia is quite dry. So the CSIRO found an insect that survived in the drier areas — the Spanish rabbit flea.

The release of the Spanish rabbit flea helped us for a while in the fight against the bunnies. But all the time, the bunnies were getting stronger and the virus was getting weaker.

In 1984, a new virus that killed only rabbits was discovered in China. This virus would kill the rabbits by causing clots in their bloodstream. Originally, this virus was called RHD (Rabbit Haemorrhagic Disease), but today it's called RCD (Rabbit Calicivirus Disease). This virus has already infected rabbits in some 40 countries around the world. It didn't seem to have any bad effects on any other animals, so it looked like it might be a good weapon to use against the bunnies in Australia.

RCD had another great advantage. It could travel directly from one rabbit to the next — it didn't need the help of an insect to carry it across.

The CSIRO brought some RCD and some rabbits to a field station on Wardang Island, off the coast of South Australia. The advantage of doing the research on an island is that it's less likely that the virus will escape. The CSIRO spent seven years testing the virus to make sure it didn't attack other Australian animals.

But the CSIRO wanted to attack the bunnies in other ways at the same time as they released the virus. They knew that sooner or later, as with the myxoma virus, the bunnies would develop a resistance to this new virus.

So, at the same time as they planned to release the RCD virus, they wanted to have a big campaign to

No Rabbits = Dead Eagles

Wedge-tailed eagles loved to eat rabbits. But as the Calicivirus swept through and killed the bunnies, the eagles had to find other food. They began to eat animals that had been killed by cars and trucks on the road.

Unfortunately, wedge-tailed eagles are big and heavy — they have wingspans of up to 2.5 metres and an average weight of around 4.5 kg. This means they are a bit slow to get off the road when a speeding car approaches. There have been reports of eagles around Broken Hill being hit by cars and smashing through the windscreen. In one case, the eagle began ripping the cabin apart as it panicked and tried to get out. There has even been one report of an eagle tearing the steel roof off a car!

rip out burrows with bulldozers, and to pump poisonous gas into the deeper burrows. They also wanted to kill the foxes and the feral cats at the same time as they released the virus. After all, if the foxes and cats liked to eat bunnies, and there were hardly any bunnies left, then the foxes and cats might start to eat native Australian animals, such as the bilby.

It was a great plan. Unfortunately, somehow the virus escaped from Wardang Island to the South Australian mainland in October 1995 and then began to spread. As it moved, it killed millions of rabbits. Although the virus had escaped too early, it seemed to be killing rabbits. There was no way we humans could stop it spreading, so the CSIRO released more of the virus around the country. In some areas, the virus killed some 90% of the rabbits.

By early 1997, the effects were remarkable. About 100 million of the 300 million rabbits in Australia had died. For the first time in living memory, there was lush vegetation on the Nullarbor Plain and in the Simpson Desert.

But would the feral cats and foxes start eating local marsupials? In Victoria, in the Hattah Lakes region, rabbits make up about 65% of the diet of feral cats, but only 15% of the diet of foxes. It's too early to tell what the feral cats and foxes will do. In Western Australia, CALM (the Department of Conservation and Land Management) has begun trying to reduce cat and fox numbers. It has already put out poisoned cat and fox baits over some 50,000 square kilometres.

Maybe this time, if we attack the bunnies on all fronts, we might be able to reduce their numbers to a manageable level.

Dung Beetle

Every hour, more than 12 million cattle dung pats (also called cattle droppings, or cattle poo) are dropped onto Australian soil. Each year, the 30 million cattle in Australia cover more than 2 million hectares of grazing land with their dung. Until recently, these cow pats would dry out slowly and stay on top of the soil for months, or even years. But thanks to imported varieties of dung beetles, these cattle droppings are now vanishing into the soil!

Cattle droppings poison the soil, because the goodness and nutrients in the dung are too concentrated. Any grass that grows around the edges of a cow pat tastes very nasty — the cattle won't eat it unless they are *very* hungry. It sounds hard to believe, but in the old days in Australia, cow pats were not biodegradable — they did not break down! When we brought cattle to Australia, we did not bring the right species of dung beetle to eat the cattle dung.

In Europe and Africa, the beetles evolved with the cattle. Wherever there were cattle making dung, there were dung beetles recycling it. The dung beetles would break down the cow dung and lay their eggs in it. So there was no problem with cattle dung in Europe and Africa. In Africa alone, there are over 2000 different species of dung beetle. Different species tend to like different environments — open pastures or woodlands, night or day, wet or dry weather, sand or clay soil, and they even prefer different seasons of the year.

Dung beetles just love fresh dung. They put the dung in their mouths, squeeze the dung and drink the juices that come streaming out. The solid parts of the dung are squeezed again in their jaws and then swallowed. If flies had laid any eggs in the dung, this squeezing action kills the eggs. Dung, along with everything else that lives in it, is the major food of the dung beetle.

In Africa, the dung beetles head for the hot, steaming cow pat even before it hits the ground. They are attracted by the gas coming out of the cow. (Each cow on our little planet lets loose 300 litres of methane gas each day, mostly as burps. Sheep produce about 20 litres of methane per day.)

Within minutes, or even seconds, the beetles are burrowing into the warm dung. Within hours, or at the very most a few days, the cow pat has vanished. All that is left is freshly turned-over soil. Scientists have counted more than 7000 busy dung beetles in a single mass of fresh elephant dung.

Most dung beetles make tunnels in the soil, under, or right next to, the dung. They shape the dung into

small balls and carry it down into the tunnels to eat later. The female lays her eggs in the dung balls. But some other dung beetles do it differently. They carve off pieces of dung, make them into smooth balls and roll these balls for many metres before they bury them. Again, the female lays eggs in the dung.

Our problems with cattle dung in Australia began with the First Fleet. In January 1788, the first English colonists to Australia brought with them five cows, two bulls, seven horses and 44 sheep.

There are native Australian dung beetles, but they are used to dealing with very small dung pellets. The largest native dung in Australia comes from the kangaroo, and it is usually much smaller than a golf ball. The huge dung pats from the imported animals just grew and grew across the land!

Some time before 1900, somebody accidentally brought one type of dung beetle, *Onthophagus depressus,* into Australia from South Africa. But it was not a success in recycling cattle dung.

In 1951, George Bornemissza, a Hungarian living in Australia, noticed something that he

Dung Beetle = Sun God

The scarab beetle, the mystical religious symbol of the ancient Egyptians, was actually a dung beetle. The Egyptians thought that the Sun rolling across the sky each day looked like a dung beetle rolling little balls of dung across the ground. They actually represented the Sun God, their most important god, as a scarab.

The Greeks also knew how important the dung beetle was. Aristophanes wrote a comedy called *The Peace*. In this comedy, Trygaeus, the hero, gets to heaven on the back of a dung beetle.

had never seen in his native Europe — fields covered with thousands of old, hard, dried cow pats. He reckoned that we needed some dung beetles from overseas to get rid of the dung.

The first dung beetles were released in April 1967 — mainly in the northern parts of Australia that were badly affected by the buffalo fly, which breeds in dung. About 275,000 dung beetles, of a few different species, were released over three years. In the early days, CSIRO scientists looked after the dung beetles like babies. They even had to carry cow dung to the hungry beetles in the backs of utilities. They called it 'Meals on Wheels'!

They were first released at spots about 80 km apart and, within two years, they had spread out and

Kids & Dung Beetles

In 1994, the Double Helix Club of the CSIRO started up 'The Dung Beetle Crusade'. All over Australia, some 1300 school kids collected dung beetles in their local area. All this information was then put onto a big map. For the first time, thanks to the kids in the Double Helix Club, the CSIRO scientists had a good idea of where the dung beetles were. They now know that at least 26 of the 50 or so species of dung beetle that were brought in have survived and are thriving.

Rebecca Scott, the Co-ordinator of the Crusade, said: 'Those Crusaders who have ... [lots] ... of dung beetles are sending a squirming parcel of beetles [by mail] to those who have none.'

filled the gaps. Gradually, the dung beetles multiplied and spread along the coast and inland. Some dung beetles can fly, and they did — to Palm Island, some 29 km off the Queensland coast!

By 1978, some 56 different species of dung beetle had been released. We need these different species of dung beetle in Australia to deal with the different climates all over the country.

There don't seem to be any disadvantages to dung beetles (but see the box opposite!). CSIRO scientists carefully looked for any problems, but they couldn't find any. After all, the cattle and the dung beetles have evolved together over millions of years.

On the other hand, there are plenty of advantages to having foreign dung beetles in Australia. Instead of lasting for up to four years, the cow pats can vanish in as little as 48 hours, especially if the climate is wet. And when they do vanish, the dung is spread evenly through the soil. The dung now acts as an excellent fertiliser, instead of poisoning the soil.

Recently, dung beetles have been given another job — cleaning up the dog poo in towns. Some people are really messy. When they take their dog for a walk and it does a poo, they don't pick it up in a plastic bag. They just leave it on the ground. They wouldn't let their children have a poo and leave it on the ground, so why do they let their dogs do it?

Dog poo in the cities is a real problem. In Sydney alone, dogs dump about 100 tonnes of poo on the ground each day! This is very bad for the environment. Dog poo is rich in phosphorus. In a

Dung Beetles – Bad

There has been at least one disadvantage to having cattle-dung beetles. One grazier said that when he laid down irrigation pipes in his fields, he would make them level by propping them up with hard, dried cattle dung. But ever since the dung beetles came into his area the cattle dung gets recycled into the soil, and he now has to carry blocks of wood with him!

big rain, the dog poo washes downhill. The phosphorus goes into creeks and kills native plants, which are not used to lots of phosphorus. Then the

Dung Beetles Without Extras

Life is everywhere. We humans each have more creatures living on our skin than there are humans on the planet (over 6 billion!). In the same way, dung beetles have little creatures living on them, such as fungi and bacteria on their outer 'skin', and nematode worms under their wing covers.

When beetles were first imported, the question was, how could we get the dung beetles into Australia without *all* their little friends? After all, it took the scientists a lot of research before they were very sure that the dung beetles would not do any harm to the Australian environment. But they couldn't be sure about all the hangers-on. So they had to get rid of them.

It was too hard to treat the living dung beetles with all the chemicals needed to kill the different types of living creatures that live on their bodies. So the scientists thought of a brilliant idea. Take some balls of Australian dung to the dung beetles in their home country. Then, get the eggs of the dung beetles (which are round and smooth and easy to clean) and wash them in chemicals that kill anything on the outside of the egg without harming the egg. Finally, put the egg inside the ball of Australian dung, bring it back to Australia, and 'hatch' the egg!

Types of Dung Beetle

There are three main types of dung beetle.

The first type burrows into the dung and lives there until the dung is all gone, or has broken down. These dung beetles are usually quite small, so they can live their entire lives inside the dung.

The second type digs a hole into the ground right next to, or underneath, the dung. These dung beetles are often large, with powerful legs. They then drag the dung down into the hole.

The third type will cut the dung into little balls, roll the balls 15 metres or more across the ground and then bury them. These dung beetles are often long and thin, with long legs. This means they can run rapidly, as well as wrap their legs around a ball of dung.

heavy rain washes the dog poo down to the ocean. There are germs (called faecal coliforms) in dog poo, and also in human poo. After a heavy rain, about half of the germs in the surf off our beaches comes from dog poo.

In 1995, Warringah Council in Sydney became the first council in Australia (and maybe the world) to use dung beetles to recycle dog poo. In November of that year, Warringah Council bought 25,000 French, North African and Spanish dung beetles.

Another good thing about dung beetles is that they can cut down the number of flies in summer. Each dung pat is a little nursery for flies — up to 3000 of them. But if the dung beetles eat the dung, there are fewer nurseries for the flies to lay their eggs in. Both the bush fly and the buffalo fly were introduced from Timor, north of Australia, in the 1890s. They lay their eggs in animal dung. Soon

Dung Beetles on Tour

The first time people deliberately took a dung beetle from one country to another for biological control was in 1906. They were trying to get rid of a fly called the 'horn fly' that lived in cattle dung in Hawaii. The Mexican dung beetle that was imported did not survive. Neither did a German dung beetle when it was brought to Hawaii in 1908. But the scientists finally succeeded in 1923 when three different species of Mexican dung beetles were imported into Hawaii and they survived. Since then, there has been a huge drop in the numbers of horn flies.

afterwards, thousands of little flies buzz away from the dung. The dung beetle breaks up the dung, buries it, and eats it. So there is less dung lying around for flies to breed in.

Research by the CSIRO in Western Australia looked at the results from having just two species of dung beetles active in their study area. (In general, most areas in Australia should have more than two species.) This research revealed that bush fly numbers had been reduced by 88%, and that survival of a bush fly egg to the adult stage had been reduced by 99%.

It seems to have worked in Canberra, according to John Feehan. He worked in the Dung Beetle

Program at the CSIRO for 25 years until it closed down in 1993. He is now a private Dung Beetle Consultant. In Canberra, after just one species of dung beetle had been introduced, the residents reported a dramatic reduction in bush fly numbers. In fact, Canberra residents can now eat outdoors in summer, without being bothered by the pestilent terror of the bush fly.

But wait — there's more! Dung beetles improve the soil as well. When they dig the dung into the soil, they make holes in the soil. This means that water can run deep into the earth and not sit around near the surface. Have you ever walked on waterlogged soil after a heavy rain and felt your feet go 'squish squish' on the ground? Well, if you had dung beetles in the area, it would take five times as much rain to waterlog, or soak, your soil.

These beetles really have got their dung together!

Wool Pressing, Twinning and Measuring

In the early days of the Australian colonies, wool was an excellent product to export. It didn't go bad like meat, so you didn't have to worry about it rotting on the long trip from the outback to the port and then across the oceans to England.

But you did have to worry about value for money. Wool is not very dense, and takes up a lot of volume. The more wool you could press into a bale, the less storage space you had to pay for, and the more money you could get for the extra wool. In those days, a bale was just a soft cotton sack stuffed full of as much wool as you could shove into it.

Thanks to the work of the merino breeders, wool exports increased very rapidly. They went from a single bale of wool in 1807, to 80 tonnes in 1821, to 6129 tonnes in 1844. So packing this wool tightly became very important.

At first the shearers would just use their own body weight, stomping and shoving the wool down into the bales, but they couldn't generate enough force this way. So a machine was invented to push the wool down.

The first machine used a heavy steel plate (called a 'monkey') attached to wire ropes to compress the wool. In 1877, this machine was greatly improved. A handle and a cog wheel were added to the monkey. So by turning the handle, you could press the wool down even more.

In 1887, a Danish mechanic called Christian Koertz came to Sydney. He worked with his partner Frederick Mason to make a whole series of improvements to wool presses. With a Koertz Press, one man working by himself could get 30 tonnes of weight to bear down on a bale of wool!

Wool presses were basically two open boxes joined with a hinge. First, you put a canvas lining into one box. Second, you put wool into both boxes. Then you swung the unlined box up, so it sat on top of the box lined with the canvas. Then the monkey plate was used to push all the wool into the

An early, highly technical,
wool pressing technique...

Big Sheep

The 1993 *Guinness Book of Records* states that the largest sheep on record weighed about 247 kg. Stratford Whisper 23H was a Suffolk ram and stood 109 cm tall. He was owned by Joseph and Susan Schallberger of Boring, Oregon, USA.

bottom box. *Voilà* — a few stitches to sew the bale shut, push it out of the box and your wool was ready to be moved out.

Thanks to the wool press we could export more wool. But to get more wool we needed more sheep. An Australian genetic scientist, Dr Helen Newton Turner, was just the person to fix this problem!

Dr Turner graduated with honours from an architecture course in 1930 — right at the beginning of the Depression. Even for such an intelligent woman, work was hard to come by during the Depression. She took a job as an architect's secretary, because that was the only work she could get at that time. A few jobs later she found herself working as a secretary at the CSIR. Her boss was Ian Clunies Ross, who was later knighted and became chairman of the CSIRO. With his help she completed the university mathematics course she was studying at night and then spent a year doing further study in England.

When she returned to Australia, she took a job as a technical officer for CSIR's McMaster Animal Health Laboratory at the University of Sydney. She was interested in merino breeding. Her earliest analysis of breeding figures showed that over 30% of the differences between sheep were inherited. It may seem obvious to us now, but back then it was very controversial. She was the first person to prove it. So, because of her research, breeders knew they could choose sheep for wool quality or wool weight or anything else they wanted, breed them together, and expect good results.

Her most famous work was proving that having twins was an inherited trait. In humans, one out of every 80 births produces a set of twins. But in sheep, the average is a bit higher — 13 sets of twins are born to every 100 merino ewes. When one CSIRO station manager at Deniliquin noticed his merinos were producing about 50 sets of twins for every 100 ewes, he knew someone should look into it!

Little Sheep

According to the 1993 *Guinness Book of Records*, the smallest breed of sheep is the Soay. These sheep are found on the island of Hirta in the St Kilda group of the Outer Hebrides, Great Britain. The adults weigh only about 25 kg.

Lots of Sheep Babies

According to the 1993 *Guinness Book of Records*, the largest number of baby lambs born at a single birth was eight (five rams and three ewes)! These babies were born in Manawatu, New Zealand, on 4 September 1991, to a Finnish Landrace ewe.

Helen Turner was that someone. She set up an experiment. She selected ewes that had borne twins, and rams that were one of a pair of twins. She mated these rams and ewes. These were her first group. In her second group, she mated ordinary rams and ewes. She compared the two groups. Her first group — the twin ewes and twin rams — had many more twins! She had proved that having twins could be inherited. As she put it, 'geneticists all around the world sat up and took notice'.

But then something even better happened. She was contacted by two brothers named Seears, of 'Booroola', near Cooma. They offered her a merino ram that had been born in a set of five. She also bought some of their ewes which had been born as one of triplets or quads. By 1972, the Booroola ewes were producing 210 lambs for every 100 births! 'Quite fantastic for merinos,' claimed Dr Turner. But there was another advantage to the Booroola ewes. They were fertile nearly all year round.

Ordinary merinos usually have a much shorter breeding season.

Every autumn, Booroola rams are sold to graziers, who can rely on their measured performance.

Dr Turner's own skills have certainly been proven. Although she officially retired from the CSIRO in 1973, she was immediately offered, and accepted, an honorary research fellowship.

Dr Turner was 20 years ahead of her time in another way. In her early days, Dr Turner had spent a lot of time thinking about ways to measure wool quality. At that time wool was bought and sold on 'look' alone. It took another 20 years before people realised that there was a need to objectively measure wool — with machines. Australian wool had been bought simply on the way it looked and felt for more than 100 years!

It was another Australian scientist who followed her ideas and changed the way in which wool was bought and sold.

It may sound ridiculous, but Dr Roy Lang spent an amazing 36 years on his experiments to measure the diameter and length of wool fibre. Lang set up a trial known as the Australian Objective Measurement Project. He showed that the diameter and length of the wool fibre was a measure of the quality of the spun wool.

There is a type of wool called 'doggy wool'. It had always been thought to be poor quality, and

The real reason it took 36 years to learn how to measure wool fibre...

Research Lab 24

I found it!!

therefore worth less than crimped wool. He showed that it was at least as good as crimped wool. This meant that farmers could charge more for doggy wool than they had in the past, and so bring more income into Australia.

New ways to breed, handle, transport, market and process wool have been based on these objective measurements, first made possible by Roy Lang.

Improvements are still being made to wool presses.

Today they are powered by electricity or petrol, not just human muscles. These new machines are much lighter than the older ones — some can even be moved by a single person. Some have a roller system to make it easier to get the bales out of the press.

Scientists are also coming up with better ways to measure different things about wool. Measuring the thickness of wool is one thing, but how can you measure the way wool will hang? How can you be sure that when you sew together the separate pieces of wool they will fit perfectly?

CSIRO came up with Sirofast Fabric Testing. This involves measuring the wool for its stretch, its thickness, its stiffness and so on. Now, people in the clothing industry can use Sirofast Fabric Testing and be sure before they start that the final product will look the way the designer wanted it to.

Wool – Fine & Coarse

Wool fibres can be skinny or fat, ranging from 16 to 40 microns thick. (A micron is a millionth of a metre, or a thousandth of a millimetre. Human hair is about 70 microns thick.)

Coarse wool fibres are fatter and longer – up to 35 cm long. Fine fibres are thinner and shorter – up to 7.5 cm in length.

Another new machine is called the Dark Fibre Detector. If you have pure white wool, just a few dark fibres can make it look terrible. It doesn't take many fibres — as little as 2 grams of dark fibres in a 175-kg bale of wool, which works out to just 0.00114% of dark fibres! The CSIRO machine can easily spot this tiny amount. This information can be used in breeding programs, to produce sheep with incredibly white wool.

In 1992, the CSIRO released another new machine to measure the thickness of wool fibres. Before this, the individual fibres had to be measured by a human using a microscope. Now a laser in the Sirolan-Laserscan Meter gives you an instant answer.

Wool is one of the oldest fibres, but it has a long future ahead of it.

Farrer — Wheat Rust

Wheat is one of the main food crops in the world. But back in the early days in Australia, wheat wasn't a reliable crop. In some years there would be a great harvest, but in other years the crop would fail. So the struggling colonies had to import wheat from overseas — and that was expensive.

The trouble was that all the varieties of wheat available at the time were best suited to European climates. They really were not suitable for the drier Australian conditions.

In some years, the crop would fail because there was not enough rain. But sometimes, in the years when there was enough rain, wheat rust would kill the wheat harvest.

The rust disease was caused by a fungus called *Puccinia graminis tritici*. The fungus made rust-coloured spots appear on the leaves and stems of the wheat and soon killed the wheat. Sometimes, the infection was so severe that even the air over the dead fields of wheat would be filled with the orange spores of the fungi. Your hair and clothes would be covered with the spores, and you would suck them into your lungs every time you breathed. This caused all sorts of health problems.

Part of the problem was that the early Australian wheat industry was not planned. Farmers planted wheat strains they had imported from overseas, without even thinking about whether they would suit Australian conditions. The farmers ended up with lots of problems, including worn-out soil, and wheat that got rust or did not tolerate dry conditions. In fact, in 1886 things were so bad that wheat rust cost the country £2 million in crop losses and wheat had to be imported.

Wheat growers were deliberately choosing varieties of wheat that would mature late in the season, because they produced bigger crops. Unfortunately, these late-maturing varieties were still growing in the fields when the rains arrived — so they were more likely to get wheat rust. Early-maturing wheat *seemed* to be more resistant to rust — but the farmers weren't really sure.

William Farrer knew about the problem of wheat rust. While he had been working as a land surveyor, he had seen the damage rust could do.

William Farrer was born in Westmoreland, England, on 3 April 1845. He graduated with

honours from Cambridge University with a degree in arts and mathematics. He began to study medicine, but could not finish the course because of health problems with his lungs. A grandson of the Reverend Samuel Marsden advised him to go to Australia because he thought the weather would be better for Farrer's health. So, in 1870, Farrer landed at Circular Quay in Sydney, aged 25.

He wanted to buy some land, so he looked around Parramatta on horseback. But his horse threw him, fracturing his skull and damaging one shoulder. For the rest of his life, one arm was lower than the other. This meant that he couldn't really do hard manual labour, so he took a job as a tutor to the children of the Campbell family, at Duntroon, near what is now Canberra. (Today, Duntroon is the site of Australia's Royal Military College.) It was there that Farrer got his introduction to farming in Australia. He saw first-hand how the wheat crops often failed, and how the millers (who ground the wheat into flour) were often forced to buy wheat from Canada.

Part of the reason for having to import flour was that many of the landowners had enormous land holdings and found it much easier to run cattle and sheep on their land than to grow crops. Even worse, the governments running the various colonies weren't really interested in growing crops either. So, in 1874, Farrer wrote a pamphlet that criticised the government of the colony of New South Wales for *a policy that paralyses all agricultural progress*. But nobody took any notice of an unknown tutor from out of town.

Farrer decided that he wanted to breed a better type of wheat, so he needed some land of his own. He took all the money that he had saved while tutoring and bought some mining shares on the stock market, hoping that they would rise in value and he could sell them for a profit. But the share price dropped and he was ruined.

He left his job as a tutor, and in 1875 took up a new job as a surveyor with the Surveyor-General's Department. He believed that one day in the future, the vast open plains around Cobar, Dubbo and Nyngan *would be covered with wheat*. But nobody believed him.

As he travelled he kept his eyes and ears open and he soon realised that the reason for the farmers' troubles was that they were still using the same few varieties of wheat that had come out on the First Fleet, almost one century earlier. He believed that the late-maturing wheat was the wrong type for this new country. He also thought that it would be possible to get an early-maturing wheat that would not only be resistant to rust when it was wet, but that would also grow in the drier areas.

In 1878, Farrer returned to England. Around that time, Charles Darwin had become interested in evolution — how one species can gradually change over generations, sometimes into another species. Darwin had just published a work called *The Effects of Cross and Self Fertilisation in the Vegetable Kingdom*, which claimed you could breed a few different plants with each other to give you a plant with quite different characteristics. If this theory was true, it meant that Farrer could 'breed' the right kind of wheat that Australia needed.

Farrer's father had died and in his will had left Farrer a regular income. This meant that Farrer didn't have to work if he didn't want to.

Farrer returned to Australia and started back at his old surveying job. In 1882, he married Nina Fane de Salis, the daughter of a Member of Parliament.

Wheat Around the World

According to the 1993 *Guinness Book of Records*, in the years 1991 and 1992, the area of land devoted over the whole world to growing wheat was some 2.22 million square kilometres (a square of land about 1490 km long on each side – roughly the distance between Alice Springs and Cairns). This land produced 541.6 million tonnes of wheat.

The largest single, fenced field to grow wheat had an area of about 142 square kilometres. It was sown in 1951, south of Lethbridge, in Alberta, Canada.

It turned out that his father-in-law owned a property on the Murrumbidgee River — Cuppacumbalong station, near Queanbeyan in New South Wales. In 1886, Farrer resigned from surveying and bought some land right next door to Cuppcumbalong. He called his farm Lambrigg.

He moved onto his land and began his life's major work — growing the best wheat for Australia. He continued his wheat-breeding experiments for the next 20 years. He set about growing many different varieties of wheat in small plots. He collected wheat from all over the world — Russia, India, Egypt, Canada, America, Europe, Arabia, Romania and Japan. He always made sure that each sample of wheat seeds came with a lot of information — how and when it grew best; what kind of rainfall it liked; what diseases affected it; what diseases didn't affect it; and how big a harvest it yielded. But he was always most interested in those varieties that had a reputation for being resistant to wheat rust.

He realised that to get the most suitable wheat strain for Australian conditions he would have to crossbreed (or marry together) different varieties of wheat. Then he could choose the healthiest and toughest plants from that generation, and crossbreed them to make the next generation of wheat — and so on. On average, he made 300 'crosses' each year, for 20 years! Of course, at every single stage, he had

Farrer's Wheat – Good & Bad

One great advantage of Farrer's varieties of wheat was that they could be grown in areas of poor rainfall. But this was also a disadvantage!

In years of no rain, the wheat crops would fail. This made no real difference for future growth if the land was undisturbed and in its original state. But, if the land had been disturbed by ploughing for wheat, in a drought year the winds would blow the topsoil away and lead to terrible erosion.

to keep very careful and accurate records, writing down every single detail. This was a huge amount of work, because crossbreeding is such a fiddly process. You have to take the pollen from the male anther of one plant and place it on the female stigma of another plant. At the beginning, Farrer didn't even have proper forceps or tweezers to carry the pollen, and he used his wife's hairpins!

But hardly anybody took him, or his work, seriously — they all thought he was mad. In one year, all his 'crosses' turned out to be useless — so he threw them all away! But he was getting closer to his goal.

Farrer's first successful cross was called Comeback. This variety of wheat had many good qualities — it matured early (so it was safe from rust), it had lots of protein (so it would make good bread) and it was resistant to drought. But it gave a small harvest, so farmers weren't keen to buy and plant it.

Farrer continued with his work and, in 1889, produced a variety he called Federation. He chose this name because people were beginning to talk of 'federation' — when Australia would turn from a bunch of colonies, controlled by England, into a single independent country. He already had a few different varieties such as Purple Straw and Yandilla that had been grown in Australia for many years. He arrived at Federation by crossing a Canadian wheat (called Fife) with an Indian wheat (called Etawah) to

Federation wheat in Australia

European wheat in Australia

get a new wheat, and then crossing this new variety with his Australian varieties.

Federation wheat took 20 years to breed. There was a lot more interest in Farrer's wheat by this time, because unfortunately for the general public and the farmers, the wheat crop of 1889 to 1890 had been destroyed by rust. Once again, the millers could not get Australian wheat and had to buy wheat from Canada.

The general public were fed up with this state of affairs. They wanted reliable food supplies, not the continuous threat of famine. The farmers were just as fed up with not having the right kind of wheat to plant for Australian conditions. They complained so much that the governments of the various colonies were forced to organise a conference about wheat. But William Farrer was not invited!

He turned up anyway and delivered a long report on his work. Everybody was very impressed. The New South Wales Government sent experts to look at his farm and his wheat.

But then he ran into another problem. Some farmers and millers claimed that his new wheat was too hard to grind in the mills — and even if it could be ground, it would not make a good bread. So Farrer teamed up with a government scientist, Dr F.B. Guthrie. Together, they worked out the best way to grind the new wheat, and even baked their own bread from it.

But people did not give him recognition for his skill and knowledge until 1896. In that year, once again, like so many times before, the Australian crop failed and the millers had to buy the expensive wheat from Canada. The millers came to think that his Federation wheat might be a good idea, after all.

Farrer could grow enough Federation seed for his little farm — but not for all of Australia. He needed to think bigger. So, when the New South Wales Department of Agriculture offered him a job in 1898 as a 'wheat experimentalist', he accepted. He didn't get much of a salary and other people stood in his way and even tried to publicly belittle him. One official said, in public, 'I would like to set a fire stick to all Farrer's crazy little wheat plots.' But the job had one great advantage — he could grow his Federation wheat in different conditions on government farms.

A Baker's Dozen Is Not 12

A baker's dozen is actually 13 loaves. Back in the old days, there were very severe cash penalties if a baker sold 'underweight' — if the weight of the bread was too little. On the other hand, it cost the baker very little to throw in an extra loaf, for safety. So the bakers began the habit of adding an extra loaf, whenever they sold a dozen loaves. This is how a 'baker's dozen' came to be 13 loaves.

Even though his work looked more and more promising, some people still didn't accept his ideas. However, Farrer wouldn't give up and, by 1902, he had enough Federation seeds to start sending them out to the farmers.

Once the farmers grew his wheat, they loved it. Farrer's dreams were proved right as his Federation wheat became a fantastic success. Federation wheat made it possible to grow wheat in parts of Australia that were previously thought useless for wheat. The amount of land that could be used to grow wheat increased rapidly — 1.4 million hectares in 1897, 4.2 million hectares in 1917, and 11 million hectares in 1991.

For the next 30 years it was *the* bestselling variety of wheat in Australia. Another attractive quality of Federation wheat was that it had short, upright ears. (The stalk of the wheat plant is the bit sticking out of the ground that you can't eat, but the ears are the bits at the top that you can eat.) These short, upright ears made it especially easy to harvest with a mechanical stripper.

Farrer was a first-class scientist and his work became well known both here and overseas. He kept very careful notes of his experiments and made sure his reports were publicised. He bred other varieties of wheat (such as Bomen, Canberra, Cleveland, Firbank, Florence and Rymer), and even successfully crossed wheat with barley (he called the cross Bobs).

The Fastest Baker's Dozen

The fastest time to bake a baker's dozen, from the living wheat growing out in the field, to the loaves hot and steaming on your plate, is 12 minutes and 11 seconds!

According to the 1993 *Guinness Book of Records*, this record was made on 23 August 1992, by people from the English villages of Clapham and Patching.

But they used 13 separate microwave ovens to cook the 13 loaves. Some people say that using a microwave oven could be 'cheating', because microwave ovens are so fast. The record using a traditional baker's oven is 19 minutes and 45 seconds, made by another English team, this time from the millers Read Woodrow, at Alpheton in Suffolk.

Farrer died on 16 April 1906, just a few days after his 61st birthday, from a heart attack. When his wife died in 1929, she was buried next to him on the hill behind their farm. In 1939, an obelisk was erected on this site. It was called the Commonwealth Farrer Memorial. In 1948, a stamp was issued in his honour.

Farrer's careful scientific work gave Australian farmers varieties of wheat that matured earlier, resisted drought and disease, produced more tonnes per hectare and were easier to harvest and mill. As a result of his work, Australia became one of the biggest wheat exporters in the world. He helped Australia feed itself and made Australia wealthier. Despite all that he did for Australia, he made little money for himself.

The wheat rust fungus is still around today. The fungus continues to change. Mostly it mutates by itself, but sometimes the fungus breeds with new spores blown in from overseas. Wheat breeders are still continuing the battle Farrer started to fight over a century ago.

Shortly before he died, Farrer said: 'I want to think that when I die my life will not have been wasted.' Thanks to his skill, hard work and wisdom his life's work has helped millions of people around the world.

Stump-jump Plough

The stump-jump plough jumps over stumps — instead of trying to cut through them. It sounds like a ridiculously simple idea, but it took thousands of years to invent. The stump-jump plough story involves a broken bolt, a vivid imagination, a hard struggle, and Robert Bower Smith.

The funny thing about Robert Smith is that slightly more than half of the books about him call him Robert, while the rest call him Richard. (So let's call him Robert.)

Robert Smith lived in South Australia. He had qualifications as an engineer, but he spent most of his life farming. His invention, the stump-jump plough, made it possible to grow crops even in the rough Australian soil.
('Plough' is also spelt 'plow'.)

In the 1800s, the hard labour of clearing the land of stumps and roots could break your back. The farmers called it 'grubbing'. Cutting down the tall timber to ground level was a hard enough job. But getting the stumps and roots out of the soil was much harder work and took a very long time. The farmers didn't like doing it, but they thought that they had to fully clear the land before they could plough it. If they couldn't plough the land, they couldn't plant a crop. And without crops to harvest and sell, the farmers had no money.

Grubbing took time and money. In fact, grubbing the land could cost seven times as much as buying it! An acre of land that cost £1 could cost £7 to clear. Cheap land could turn out to be very expensive!

In the 1800s, the farmers had hardly any machinery to help them. There was a very rough plough called the 'Mulleniser' — it was probably their most sophisticated machine. The Mulleniser, of course, was invented by a farmer called Mullens. The Mulleniser was really just a log in the shape of a 'V' with tough spikes hammered into the bottom of the log. The Mulleniser was simply dragged around by a horse hitched to the point of the 'V'.

The advantage of the Mulleniser was that it could open the ground even in an ungrubbed paddock. Because the Mulleniser was so rough and tough, mere stumps wouldn't stop it. So Farmer Mullens got crops to grow quickly, even in rough ground. And, once the crops had grown, even though the ground was rough, he could use a stripping machine to harvest his crops.

The big problem was that Mullenising was not very good for the soil. It was certainly never as good as ploughing.

The plough is the most important agricultural tool invented in the history of the human race. The first

History of the Plough

Plants were grown as a food crop 13,000 years ago, in what is now Thailand. Ten thousand years ago, food crops were grown in the area that is Iran, Iraq and Syria today.

The earliest known plough was used by the Egyptians and the Norwegians, over 4000 years ago. Artists from Babylon have left us a picture of a plough from the Nile Valley drawn in 2100 BC. It had a metal tip to cut through the soil. It even had a bamboo container to drop seeds into the freshly cut furrow in the soil.

The next major improvement was the plough that the invading Angles and Saxons brought into Britain. It had a mouldboard and share, and was guided by two long handles. It even had two wheels mounted on an axle to take some of the load off the horses or oxen pulling it.

tool used as a plough was probably a simple digging stick. A plough is used to turn the soil over, breaking it up. At the same time, it can bury the remants of the last season's crops and control weeds.

A ploughshare is a ploughing blade and is part of the machinery designed to cut the groove into the soil. The 'share' is the point that digs through the soil. Originally, the share was made out of a very hard wood which had been toughened by putting it into a flame. Today, the share is made of cast iron or steel.

The ploughshare is mounted on a section of the machinery that is called a mouldboard. The mouldboard is usually curved, so that it can lift up the dirt that has been dug by the share and push it over to one side. So the share and mouldboard work together to make a groove in the soil.

At first, the mouldboard and the share were a fixed part of the frame. A curved iron bar connected the mouldboard to the frame, which was pulled by an animal or, when times were bad, people! The curved iron bar was bolted onto the mouldboard by two bolts.

There was one major problem with having the mouldboard and share *rigidly* attached to the frame. If the share ran into a buried stump, or its roots, one of three things could happen. First, the whole plough could come to a sudden, shuddering halt. This could hurt the animals. Second, the share and mouldboard assembly could break. This would stop the ploughing until the plough was fixed. Third, if you were very lucky, the share might cut right through the root and you could keep on ploughing.

Robert Smith's invention of the stump-jump plough was the first major change to the original plough design. It was one of Australia's greatest early inventions in the field of agriculture. It meant that land that had been regarded as useless could be put to work growing food crops for the young country.

In the late 1870s, Smith was a poor farmer. He had a young family to support. Every day he worked hard on his land.

One day, while he was out ploughing, one of the bolts holding the mouldboard of his plough to the frame broke. But he kept on ploughing, because he could not afford to lose a day's work. He was hoping to get a little bit more done before the plough broke down completely.

Smith expected the broken plough to break down almost immediately — but it didn't, and he was very surprised. And what's more, it didn't stall. Normally, the share smashed into any stumps or rocks left behind in the paddock and came to a juddering halt.

But thanks to the broken bolt, this wasn't happening. Instead, the share and mouldboard assembly was lifting up over the scattered rocks and stumps. Once it was over the obstacle, the weight of the share and mouldboard assembly made it dive back into the soil to keep on digging the furrow. Smith's genius lay in understanding what he had just seen. To Robert Smith the plough looked as if it were *jumping* over the buried *stumps*.

The broken bolt was the idea behind Smith's development of the stump-jump plough. He realised that if the plough could 'jump' over the stumps, then you didn't have to grub the land before ploughing! This would be a great thing in the mallee country of Victoria and South Australia, where digging out mallee roots was a terrible task.

Robert Smith worked with his brother Clarence, an apprentice blacksmith, to design and build a stump-jump plough. Robert attached a protective bar, a 'coulter', to the bar holding the mouldboard. The point of the coulter was a few centimetres below and in front of the share. The coulter would help to protect the tip of the share from buried rocks.

He also added a lever arm which carried a 25-kg weight. This arm would force the mouldboard and share back into the soil after they had jumped over a stump. The farmer could slide the weight along the arm to increase or decrease the force that would bring the mouldboard and share down again.

Their first working model was finished in June 1876. It was called the 'Vixen' and had three shares, so it could make three furrows at the same time.

In that same year, Smith's earlier model of a one-furrow stump-jump plough won first prize at the Moonta Agricultural Show on the Yorke Peninsula in South Australia.

Robert Smith put all of his money into producing the best possible stump-jump plough. He didn't have any money left over — not even enough to buy clothes! — but Smith didn't worry. He thought his idea would be a winner.

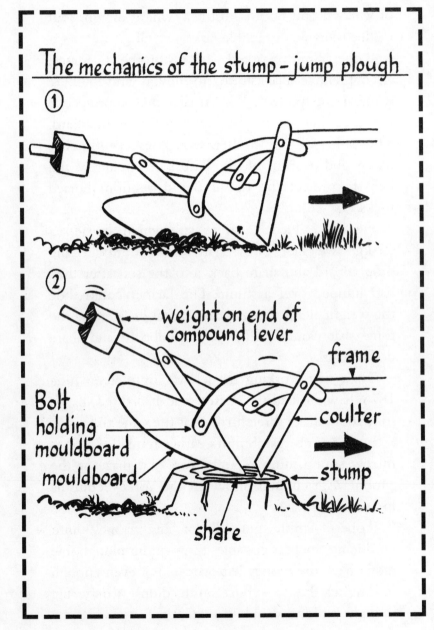

The mechanics of the stump-jump plough

①

② weight on end of compound lever

frame

Bolt holding mouldboard

coulter

mouldboard

stump

share

Unfortunately, other farmers didn't share his vision. They laughed at the wonderful new stump-jump plough. They made out that Smith was crazy. Maybe the farmers lacked common sense; maybe their Anglo-Saxon work ethic was too rigid for their own good. 'It's sloppy to plough the soil before you clear the stumps,' they said, even though the stump-jump plough made clearing an unnecessary step. They also said that the stump-jump plough 'would only tickle the surface of the soil', and 'would be all right for a slovenly farmer — fancy seeding while stumps are still in the ground'. They believed in 'getting the land clear first, even if it does take a few years'. They couldn't see that the stump-jump plough would save them years of heavy work grubbing the land.

Even Clarence Smith, Robert's own brother and assistant, wrote to him and said: *I hope your plough is all right after all this but I am afraid it is not.*

In spite of all this bad feeling, Robert Smith went ahead. On 19 February 1877, he took out a one-year patent on the stump-jump plough. This was before Federation. So he had to pay each of the six states for a separate patent. This was quite an expensive process.

In the following year, things didn't improve much for Robert Smith, certainly not in money terms, anyway. Smith was very depressed.

He even wrote to a friend saying: *My invention has cost me some money, some anxiety and condemned my*

Ploughing Records

According to the 1993 *Guinness Book of Records*, the fastest time for ploughing an acre of land (about 0.404 hectare) is nine minutes and 49.88 seconds. On 21 October 1989, Joe Langcake at Hornby Hall Farm, Brougham, England, set this record using a Case IH 7140 Magnum tractor and a Kverneland four-furrow plough.

The greatest area plowed in 24 hours, to a depth of 9 inches (about 230 mm), is 173 acres (about 70 hectares, or 0.7 square kilometres). Richard Gaisford and Peter Gooding set this record on 25 to 26 September 1990, at Manor Farm, Pewsey, England, with a Case IH tractor and a Lemken plough.

little ones to all the miseries of poverty and banishment to the bush. If I had been a successful cricketer, good bowler, or a rifle shooter, without pluck, a Blondin [a famous tightrope walker] or an acrobat, I and mine would have escaped these ills.

In 1878, the stump-jump plough patents expired. Robert Smith couldn't afford to renew them. This meant anyone could come along and take his ideas for their own benefit — without giving Smith any money or credit.

In fact, this is exactly what happened. Even Clarence jumped onto the bandwagon. After all the discouraging things he had said to his brother early on, Clarence then put quite a few years into improving the stump-jump plough.

With time, people finally came to realise what a clever and simple invention the stump-jump plough was. At last people admitted that it could really help the farmer.

Even a parliamentarian, Robert Ross, began thinking about Smith's stump-jump plough. He thought that the government should offer Smith some kind of payment, a reward for all his work. (At this time, Smith was just about bankrupt.) Ross provoked an awful lot of parliamentary debate. Once he started talking about a reward, he also provoked a lot of other people into claiming that they had invented the stump-jump plough.

In 1882, Parliament made a decision. They awarded Robert Smith £500, 260 hectares of land at Ardrossan in South Australia and a gold medal.

Robert used his money to go back into business with his brother at Ardrossan. They continued the work of improving the stump-jump plough. But Clarence died while still young — at only 45. Robert continued building stump-jump ploughs at his factory in Ardrossan and lived until he was 81.

Soon after Clarence died, the people of Ardrossan erected a plaque in memory of Clarence — honouring him as the person responsible for the stump-jump plough! Robert protested bitterly, but to no avail. The marble memorial plaque giving credit to Clarence for Robert's work went ahead as planned.

Smith's stump-jump plough changed farming practice all over the world. In Australia and America the stump-jump plough was a great success. But in his own town, in his lifetime, he was not recognised.

Rainforests

Faster than a speeding bullet ... the world's tropical rainforests are being cut down at a rate of about 10 to 25 hectares a minute. At this rate, in just a century or so, there won't be any rainforest left.

Most of the 2 billion hectares of tropical rainforest left in the world is found in the developing countries. These countries are poor. They are often overpopulated, and the people often live in very crowded conditions. The pressure on the people to chop down rainforests in these countries is huge. Cutting down the rainforest has two advantages for them — wood to sell as timber or wood chips, and more land to live on.

This means Australia has a very special role in preserving our rainforests. We are a wealthy, well-educated nation. We can certainly afford to save our rainforests for the future.

Rainforests are very different from other forests. They are sometimes called 'closed forests'. This is because they have a cover or canopy over them, which may be as high as 30 to 50 metres above the ground. The canopy is just like our skin — it protects what is underneath. Underneath the canopy are thousands of plants and animals.

More than half of all the species of plants and animals in the world are found in rainforests! In just a tiny patch of rainforest (only 100 square metres) in the Atherton Tablelands in far north Queensland, scientists have found 164 different species of trees.

In a rainforest the plants are arranged in layers. There are always at least three layers of plants — one is the canopy, one is on the ground and one is in between these two. The plants in a rainforest depend on each other for survival. You can't cut one rainforest tree down without affecting the whole of the forest. And rainforests don't grow back quickly — once you've cut a hole in a rainforest the hole is soon filled up with weeds. The weeds then spread further into the rainforest and destroy more of it!

Rainforests seem very lush, but this isn't because they grow on very rich soil. In fact, rainforests often grow on very poor soil! Rainforests look so good because they fertilise their own soil. They recycle dead trees and leaves quickly, and the rest of the rainforest can use these nutrients. So cutting down the forest means you destroy this way of putting goodies back into the soil — and you get left with the original crummy dirt.

Of the rainforest in Australia, 55% is in Queensland, 32% in Tasmania, 11% in New South Wales and 1% in Victoria. Most of the plants in our rainforests are at risk of extinction. And we still know so little about rainforests. A report in 1980 by the United States Academy of Science says that we probably know of only one-sixth of the 3 million species of plants and animals living in tropical forests. This is a real worry, if we destroy rainforests without knowing what is in them first.

Australia has three types of rainforest. These are tropical, subtropical and temperate. Tropical rainforest

Rainforests have given us...

pepper   rubber   tea   coffee   chocolate

Drugs from Rainforest Plants

Common crops like rubber, tea, coffee, chocolate and pepper originally came from rainforests.

Also, many drugs come from rainforests. A little pink flower called the Madagascar periwinkle is used to make drugs to treat leukaemia in children. Before the drugs in the periwinkle were discovered, all the kids who got leukaemia died within five years. But now, about half of the kids who get leukaemia survive for more than five years, because of the drugs in the Madagascar periwinkle.

The steroid part of a contraceptive pill comes from two Australian native plants, *Solarum aviculare* and *Solarum laciniatum*. The contraceptive pill is used by women to stop them from getting pregnant. Oddly, it is the Soviet Union, not Australia, that has planted these species for crops. So it is the Soviet Union that makes more than a billion dollars every year out of growing and selling the steroid.

The seeds of another Australian native, *Castanospermum*, or black bean, have recently been studied by American researchers. Scientists have found this plant can stop the growth of one type of cancer cell. Unfortunately, the black bean has been mostly cut down by loggers. Killing off whole species like this means we are throwing away many future medical breakthroughs.

grows in Queensland, between Cape York and Ingham. Subtropical rainforest is found between

Mackay and Kiama on the east coast. The temperate rainforest is found in Victoria and Tasmania and is mostly made up of Antarctic beech. Rainforest in Australia is usually surrounded on all sides by eucalypts, so it ends up being a bit like an island.

Plants form the basis of life on our planet. Ninety-five per cent of all the world's food comes from just 30 plants. In fact, just eight plants make up about three-quarters of our diet. Yet there are over 80,000 plants growing around the world that, potentially, we could eat. Fuel, medicines, paper and building wood also come from plants.

In 1944, the CSIRO set up the world's first study of rainforests. It was headed by Dr Len Webb. He was looking for important drugs like morphine, penicillin, cocaine and strychnine that might be extracted from the plants in the rainforest.

Len Webb went into the forest to collect the leaves, barks and roots of plants. To help him choose useful plants, he read medical textbooks and listened to stories from the bushmen, graziers and timber workers. He also learnt about Aboriginal bush medicine. By the 1950s, he had found 500 drugs. Some 200 of these drugs were brand-new to science. You're ten times more likely to find a valuable plant in a rainforest than in the ordinary bush. Rainforests are like an Aladdin's Cave.

Len Webb joined up with another CSIRO scientist, Geoff Tracey. They made an Australia-wide map of rainforests and set up a whole new system of describing rainforests. Before then, rainforests were described according to the species of plants found in them, but the trouble with that system was that the rainforest was so complex nobody knew even a tenth of its plants.

Their new system described rainforests by the way the forest looked. For example, they collected information about the size of the leaves, and whether the leaves fell off in winter or stayed on the tree all year round. Webb and Tracey then matched the way the rainforest canopy and the leaves looked, with how abundant certain plants were, with the type of soil in the area, and with the climate. All this information let them quickly classify the rainforest. It was then easy to compare one type of rainforest with another.

Their system is better than the previous system, but it doesn't consider any of the animals in the rainforest. Nor does it look at how the animals affect the rainforest, and vice versa.

Weapons from Rainforests

Defence forces around the world are also looking at the rainforest. What they want are irritant plants — they're not looking for medicines, they're looking for weapons. They want more chemicals to use for biological warfare.

Drugs from Rainforest Animals

Even rainforest animals can produce valuable drugs.

One of the most lucrative drugs in the world is one that treats stomach ulcers. When someone has stomach ulcers, the acid in the stomach actually begins to eat into the stomach wall.

There was a rainforest frog that swallowed its own fertilised eggs, and turned its stomach into a temporary womb or uterus. Somehow, the frog stopped the acid in its stomach from eating at its own eggs.

Unfortunately, we can never use the frog's trick to stop the acid in people's stomachs from eating into the stomach lining – because the frog is now extinct.

Len Webb and Geoff Tracey also put forward a whole new set of theories about where Australia's rainforests came from. Scientists used to believe that Australia's rainforests were inherited from Southeast Asia. They thought that the rainforests spread down across a land bridge from Asia into Australia before the continents drifted apart.

Webb and Tracey now believe that Australia was a major centre where primitive flowering plants evolved or changed. Australian rainforests have two primitive plant families that occur nowhere else in the world.

Clean Streams in Rainforests

Whenever you go into a rainforest, you'll notice that the streams you see are incredibly clean. They have very pure drinking water.

This is because the trees' roots suck out all the nutrients, leaving behind pure water. This is an example of how good a rainforest is at recycling. The water leaves the rainforest, and so the rainforest pulls all the possible nutrients out of the running water before it goes.

These plants are not found anywhere in Asia, so could not have spread down to Australia from there.

Other evidence that the rainforests are native to Australia has come from fossils. Dr Helen Martin of the University of New South Wales has found fossils of rainforest pollens. These fossils show that rainforests were present in Australia 70 million years ago. This is before the drift of the land masses could have bought Asia close enough to Australia for any plant migration to occur.

In 1788, rainforests covered only 1% (about 8 million hectares) of Australia. They didn't cover a lot of area, and their timbers (especially from hoop pine and red cedar trees) were heavily used in making houses.

Since then, modern methods of logging, mining and farming, clearing for housing and damage by tourists have caused the rainforest area to drop to about 2 million hectares. This is a loss of 75%.

Back then, the new settlers to Australia couldn't see the value of rainforests. Rainforests had no grasses for their horses or cattle and the soil looked lush. The trees were easily cleared (because of their shallow roots) — so they were. Today we know that a rainforest, unlike other forests, holds most of its

Our future is getting clearer and clearer...

nutrients in the trees, not in the soil. So once you cut down the trees, you're left with poor soil. The native rainforest trees also have special fungi living in their roots, to help them get the very last bit of nutrition out of the soil. The crops that the early settlers planted didn't have these special fungi. They got only a few crops from the soil before it was useless.

The potential of the rainforest is great. There are still many unknown drugs, plants and animals in rainforests. But rainforest is scarce. Unless we protect it today we'll never be able to know — let alone use — its value in the future!

Wool Spinning & Flammability

Since the days when the first sheep were brought into Australia, many men and women have worked hard and cleverly to breed better sheep — succeeded. By 1960, Australia was a world leader in producing sheep and wool.

But, now there were new problems.

First, synthetic fibres were coming onto the market. In some ways, these fibres had advantages over the natural fibres like wool and cotton. For example, a synthetic fibre won't usually shrink when it's washed, but wool can shrink in the wash. Wool has to be treated or changed, so that it has properties that will not be affected by washing.

econd, the technology of spinning wool had reached a technological roadblock. It was impossible to make the spinning machines go any faster. The easy, but foolish, way would have been to build more spinning machines, but what we really needed was a whole new way of thinking.

It was a CSIRO physicist, David Henshaw, who came up with a totally new way to spin wool. Australians are often said to have little respect for tradition — and maybe this worked in David Henshaw's favour!

When you cut the fleece off a sheep, you end up with a blob of tangled wool fibres that is not really very useful in its raw state. You have to spin it to get a thread. The easiest way to spin wool is to pluck out a thread, pull gently and evenly on it, and wind it onto a stick — which you then rotate with your fingers and thumb. If you do it this way, winding the thread straight onto the stick, there's no 'twist' or 'spiral' to the thread.

However, there are certain advantages to having a twisted thread. For example, the individual fibres that make up the thread get 'locked' into each other by friction, as they get twisted around each other. When you pull on the thread, the individual fibres drag on each other, spreading the load. Having this friction makes the thread stronger and less likely to break.

So, if you want a twist, you have to spin the stick

like the second hand on a watch. But turning the wool onto a stick by *hand* is a slow way to spin the thread.

Thousands of years ago, somebody (probably from India) invented the spinning wheel. The spinning wheel has the blob of wool mounted on a stick and the thread coming onto the outside of a wheel. Here it's the stick (which has the blob of wool on it) that spins like the second hand on a watch.

The knowledge of the spinning wheel travelled overland to the Middle East, and arrived in Europe in the Middle Ages. At first, the wheel was turned by hand, but later it was rotated by pressing a foot pedal.

The next big invention was the 'Spinning Jenny', which is just a bunch of spinning wheels working together.

A traditional spinning wheel

In 1764 (so the popular story goes), Jenny Hargreaves, the daughter of James Hargreaves, accidentally tipped a spinning wheel on its side.

James noticed that the wheel kept

on spinning and that it still worked perfectly well. He suddenly realised that if he could stack up eight spinning wheels on top of each other, this new machine could spin wool eight times faster.

You can see the need for a faster way to spin when you realise that it takes about 20 km of yarn to make a suit!

In honour of his daughter, James called his new machine the Spinning Jenny. It spun 15 metres of yarn per minute.

Unfortunately, the thread made by a Spinning Jenny was not very strong. In fact, the thread was suitable only as a filling or stuffing material. Other British inventors, Sir Richard Arkwright (1769) and Samuel Compton (1779), came up with improvements to the original Spinning Jenny that made it spin a stronger thread. An operator using Compton's machine could control 1000 spinning wheels at the same time!

But still the spinning machine was limited to a certain top speed. There was a spindle which turned to spin the wool. The fastest you could turn this spindle was 10,000 revolutions a minute. If it spun any faster than that, the centrifugal force would be too great. (The centrifugal force is the force that kids feel when parents spin them around while holding onto their hands. This force makes the kids feel like they would fly outward if their parents let go of their hands.) When the centrifugal force was too big, the wool would snap. Apparently, spinning machines could only spin so fast and no faster. The thread was always spun in the one direction. Nobody in the whole world could work out a way to spin wool faster.

But on Wednesday 8 February 1961, David Henshaw, a scientist from the CSIRO Textile Division in Geelong, had a fantastic idea! He was sitting in the library. He had realised that conventional spinning technology had run into a dead-end. Being a bit of a lateral thinker, 'Why waste time mucking around with a machine that is already going as fast as it can?' he asked himself, What he decided to do was to make a new type of yarn.

He threw away the notion of having to spin the yarn in the one direction. His idea was to take two

Longest Wool Thread

According to the 1993 *Guinness Book of Records*, the longest single thread of wool was some 553.29 metres long and grown in Australia. This thread weighed 9.92 grams and was shown at the International Highland Spin-in at Bothwell, Tasmania, on 1 March 1989. It was hand-spun by Julitha Barber of Bull Creek, Western Australia.

bits of yarn and pin them together at one end. The strands were held apart. Each strand was twisted separately in the same direction. When he lay the strands side by side and then let go, an amazing thing happened. The strands wrapped back around each other. You can do this experiment at home.

This idea was so easy and it became the basis of all the new wool spinning machines. The thread could be spun at very high speeds, because all you needed to do was twist a skinny thread, instead of rotating a big wheel. Even though the thread was spun using a new technology, it was just as strong as thread made the old way with Compton's machine.

Crimped Merino Wool

The wool fibres of the merino are not straight, but crimped. Fine wool fibres have about 12 'waves' in each centimetre, while coarse wool fibres have less than two waves per centimetre.

The advantage of this waviness is that the fibres have natural air spaces between them. This air is an excellent insulator.

Another advantage is that the wool fibres stick together. So even yarns that are made of loosely intermingled fibres are still strong.

Wool & Creases

One great advantage of wool is that you can rumple it and it won't crease. This is very handy when you pack woollen clothes into a suitcase. But this lack of creasing can be a disadvantage. What if you want to put a permanent crease into a woollen garment? In 1958, CSIRO scientists invented Siroset. This process puts a permanent pleat into the garment, while the wool still keeps its advantage of being elastic and not getting wrinkled.

When you looked at the thread, you could see a long section with a clockwise twist, then a short section with no twist, and then a long section with an anticlockwise twist, another short section with no twist, then a clockwise twist, and so on. So the new thread was spun in two directions.

One problem was the short sections with no twist. Easy — he just gave the whole yarn another slight twist and now every bit of the thread was twisted.

Because this yarn was made from two separate threads, it was called a 'two-ply' yarn.

With his colleagues, Gordon Walls and Basil Ellis, Henshaw set about building a machine that could spin this new yarn for businesses. The CSIRO asked Repco Limited to help them with the project.

It took the team two years to design and build the machine. It used two rollers which rotated, just like the old-fashioned wringer washing machine. The rollers pushed out the yarn — but they also moved from side to side. So the two strands of wool were twisted by the sideways action — first one way, then the other. The twisted strands of wool were allowed to come together and untwist around each other as they came out of the rollers.

The first generation of the Repco self-twist spinner could produce 220 metres of yarn a minute. That was 11 times faster than the old machines. It was also quieter, smaller (it took up only one-third of the space of the old machines), and used less power to run (only 60% of previous machines). It also needed a lot less maintenance to keep it running well.

In 1970 the Repco Spinner won the Prince Philip Prize for Industrial Design. The judges were very impressed by this machine. They said: *The spinning machine is as revolutionary in design as is the process that it employs. The designers have produced a compact piece of equipment of first-class finish, elegant and aesthetic in appearance, incorporating engineering principles not previously applied in the textile machinery field. Particularly notable is the mounting of the self-twist rollers on an air-cushion which allows almost frictionless motion both of rotation and reciprocation. Equally ingenious is the actuating mechanism which produced both these motions through the one linkage. In fact, great ingenuity has been displayed.*

Henshaw and Walls had the first suits ever made out of the new self-twisted yarn. They even made the then Prime Minister, Sir Robert Menzies, some clan Menzies tartan curtains for his study from the new yarn! (There was so much secrecy about the new spinning process that not even Sir Robert Menzies was told what was so special about his new curtains!)

In 1975 Repco brought out an improved machine, called the 'SELFIL Spinner'. The SELFIL machine produces a yarn that is perfect for knitting. It uses a core of wool and wraps two thin nylon strands around it. This incorporation of 20% synthetic makes the yarn very strong.

The SELFIL Spinner, like the earlier Repco Spinner, won the Prince Philip Prize for Industrial Design. But the designers didn't stop there. In 1980, an improved version of this technology, Sirospun, was introduced.

Being able to spin wool faster was only the first of the changes that Australia had to come up with. We also had to change, and improve, the character of wool. One such change was to make wool more flame-proof.

One problem with most synthetic materials is that they burn very easily, and that they melt, and then 'shrink' away from the flame. This means that they give no insulation or protection to the wearer.

Wool is virtually non flammable...

But wool has a natural advantage — it's hard to set alight and the burning process tends to stop once you take away the flame.

The wool industry is lucky to have had a man like Tom Pressley working for it. Pressley worked in the CSIRO's Division of Protein Chemistry and was very interested in textile flammability.

When Qantas wanted to use wool seat covers for their very first Boeing 747s in 1971, they had to call in Tom Pressley. The Boeing Company was very concerned that wool would not be able to pass the 'Vertical Burn Test' of the United States Federal Aviation Administration. This test involves holding a flame for 12 seconds against a piece of material. To pass the test no more than 20 cm of the fabric can have been burnt, *and* the material must stop burning by itself within 15 seconds of removing the flame. Pressley proved that wool treated with a fireproofing treatment perfected by CSIRO would pass the test. So Qantas went ahead and installed soft and comfortable

Wool & Shrinking

One problem with woollen garments is that they can shrink in the wash. Two processes have been invented by Australians to make wool shrink-proof.

Chlorine Hercosett was invented in 1967. In this process, a resin is used to treat the fibres and, during a heating stage, actually leaves a thin film on all the fibres of wool. This stops little scales on the wool from reaching out and tangling with other little scales. If the scales don't tangle, the wool is less likely to shrink.

A better process, Sirolan BAP, was invented in 1977. In this process, two synthetic resins are impregnated into the wool fibres and then allowed to dry. As they dry, the resins make links between the fibres of wool. This means that the fibres can't easily move closer together — and shrink.

wool seat covers. On 16 August 1971, the first Qantas jumbo, the *City of Canberra*, had its very first flight with the new wool on its seats.

Pressley often said, 'Science is simply common sense.' But it's often hard work, too.

Another of Pressley's projects was persuading the Royal Melbourne Hospital *not* to throw out all their wool blankets. A hospital doctor was convinced that the wool blanket fluff was floating through the air and spreading a really nasty bacteria called golden staph. Pressley showed that 96% of the fibres in the air were from cotton, and, anyway, the bacteria wasn't spread by fibres floating in the air at all! Not bad for a scientist who at first knew nothing about infection: 'For all I knew, you caught microbes in a butterfly net.'

But he hadn't finished his work with wool. He went on to develop a way to boil blankets, to kill bacteria, that did not shrink the blankets. The shrink-resistant part worked fine, but the blankets went a dirty, rusty colour and felt very rough after just a few washes. Pressley found it was iron in the water making everything go brown. He fixed that with a chemical that stuck to the iron, and stopped it getting into the wool.

To make the wool feel softer, he even invented a new detergent. He sold the formula to Unilever and they called it — you guessed it! — 'Softly'!

Australian inventors just keep on coming up with new ways to improve wool. This means wool can now compete with synthetic fibres. Thanks to Australian ingenuity, wool can now be made shrink-proof, flame-proof, permanently pleated, and even lightweight and cool for summer!

The wool story is certainly one where Australia has kept on keeping on!

Sheep Shearing

Australia has more sheep than any other country in the world. In 1990, we had 177.8 million. Sheep give us two main products — wool and meat. In the days before Australia developed its other industries, sheep gave us a huge percentage of our income. Sheep were so important to our economy that people used to say: 'Australia rides on the sheep's back.'

To get the wool, you have to shear the sheep. Shearing sheep by hand is hard and sweaty work. The whole day is spent hunched over the animal, opening and closing the shears until your hands and wrists ache. Hand shears are just like two big knife blades riveted together.

Back in the days before machine shears were invented, it took two years of training, plus experience on the job, to become a skilled hand shearer. A good shearer could get through about 200 sheep a day. In fact, shearers were paid according to the number of sheep they had shorn by the end of the day, so the pressure was always on to work faster.

Australia's sheep population grew rapidly — from a few thousand sheep in 1800 to more than 100 million in 1900. Wool was Australia's biggest export. The sheep owners were interested in anything that would get the sheep shorn more quickly and cheaply. When mechanical shears were invented, the sheep farmers were very keen to adopt the new machines to increase their profits.

The shearers had a completely different point of view! A shearing machine meant that anyone could learn to be a skilled shearer in just a few days — very different from the years of training they had had to go through. Shearers were worried that they would soon be out of jobs. That's why they fought so hard against the introduction of shearing machines.

In 1868, James Hingham from Victoria was the first to patent a sheep-shearing machine. The idea for his machine came from a British machine that would clip horsehair. Clipping horses and shearing sheep were two very different activities, so his machine had problems. A major problem was that the shearing machine was fixed in one spot. This made it difficult to use with a live, wriggling sheep!

In the days before small electric motors, the only way to get power for such a machine was from a big steam engine. The steam engine turned a large shaft, which in turn fed power down to a number of machines in a building.

This steam engine was usually outside the shed or factory. Running just under the roof of the building was a huge shaft, as long as the entire building. On the outside of the building, the steam engine was connected to the shaft by a wide leather belt. (This

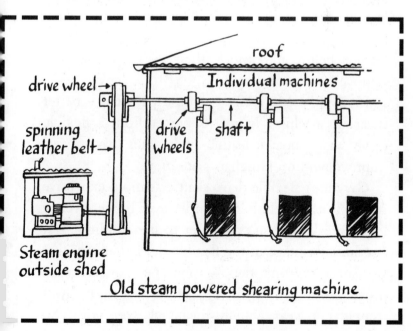

Old steam powered shearing machine

was before rubber was in common use.) As the steam engine worked, it turned the huge shaft. Inside the building, there were many smaller leather belts running from the shaft down to individual machines. This process allowed workers to run many different machines from just one steam engine. The disadvantage of this system was that when the leather belt broke, which happened quite often, there was a great risk to the workers. The flying leather belt could knock their eyes out, or even remove an arm or a leg.

In 1870, a Mr J.A.E. Gwynne patented a better shearing machine. It got its power from a flexible drive shaft, not a leather belt. This was a real improvement on Hingham's attempt.

Gwynne's flexible drive shaft was more expensive than a leather belt, but it hardly ever broke. Even if it did break, it wasn't a danger to life and limb. But another advantage of the flexible drive shaft was that the shearer wasn't tied to one spot — he could move around. The drive shaft was driven by a straight-cut gear, which meant it was noisy. So

Gwynne then cut the gears with rounded edges to make them a bit quieter.

But it was Frederick York Wolseley and Robert Savage who actually got the first commercially successful shearing machine up and running. By 1872, their first rough models were already getting the wool off sheep's backs.

In 1854, when he was only 17 years old, Wolseley came from Ireland to Australia. (He later went back to England to found the Wolseley car firm! He designed a gyrocar like Louis Brennan — see 'Australian Torpedo and Monorail' in *Ears, Gears & Gadgets*.) It was probably his first job as a jackeroo — a general station hand — that got him interested in sheep shearing. Wolseley was helped with his sheep-shearing machine by another man called Herbert Austin. (Austin was also involved with the Wolseley car firm. When Wolseley died, Austin branched off and made his own car, the 'Austin'.)

Wolseley worked with many different tradespeople to modify and improve his shearing machine. They eventually made a model that used the old system of a steam engine to turn an overhead shaft. But it didn't use a leather belt or a gear mechanism to bring power down to the shearers' equipment on the shop floor. The drive mechanism pressed a cone against a large wheel on the shaft in the ceiling. As the cone rotated, so did the flexible drive shaft.

By 1877, the machine worked well enough to be patented. There was a comb to run through the wool and a cutting blade that moved sideways behind the comb. But it took until 1885 to get it to be more efficient than hand shears and to increase its reliability.

To make people interested in his machine, Wolseley organised a big sheep-shearing demonstration. This was held in a Melbourne store. To make it more exciting, they turned the display into a competition. The competition was between a gun hand shearer called Dave Brown and two machine shearers — Hassam Ali and Jack Joy.

Wolseley's heart was in his mouth at the end of the race, because it was Dave Brown, the hand shearer, who finished first! If it hadn't been for Ali's quick thinking, the shearing machine would probably never have been accepted. Even though Ali had already been declared the loser, he ran his mechanical shears over Dave Brown's hand-shorn sheep. An extra third of a kilo of wool came off each sheep! The shearing machines were more thorough, even if they weren't quicker.

David Wilson was impressed by this demonstration. He managed Dunlop, a huge property near Bourke. Wilson ordered 40 machines for the property. Then he picked out 40 of the best shearers to use them.

The shearers from Dunlop were furious! They declared an immediate strike. Wilson was stuck with

184,000 unshorn sheep on his property on one side of the flooded Darling River. On the other side of the river were the angry shearers, in a makeshift camp.

Every day, two men from the station (John Howard, the mechanic who helped Wolseley, and Charlie Shepherd) visited the striking workers. For three weeks the shearers refused to negotiate with them. The shearers were very upset by two things — they were scared of being put out of work by the

Hand shearing Vs Machine shearing

machines and they were very angry about being expected to supply their own combs and cutters for the machines.

The talks were getting nowhere. It wasn't until John Howard accepted a daredevil bet from the striking shearers to swim the flooded river that any progress was made. Howard made it across the river without drowning — some people even say twice! After this the shearers decided he was a 'good bloke' — and, in return, they agreed to give the shearing machines a go.

But they still had problems with using the machines. At first the shearers were shearing only 50 sheep a day, and much of the equipment was being deliberately broken. Neither side was very happy.

After a while the shearers got sick of this situation. Jim Davidson, a gun hand shearer, decided to try hard at the machines. By the fourth day of his trial, he had shorn 114 sheep. With each day his total got higher and higher. He set the pace for the rest of the shed! Once they knew how to use the new machines efficiently, the shearers got very fast.

After this, Wolseley's machines were installed in shearing sheds all over the country. Jim Davidson became involved in promoting the machines. Eventually, it became normal to use the shearing machines rather than the hand shears.

The day may yet come when a shearer's services are not needed at all (which is what shearers were worried about from the beginning). Various people are developing a robot to shear sheep. It's hard work to shear a sheep and lots of shearers get back injuries. The sheep may not actually kick, but it's a

Big Sheep Numbers

According to the 1993 *Guinness Book of Records*, the world's largest sheep farm is Commonwealth Hill in South Australia. It has some 222 km of dog-proof fencing surrounding some 10,567 square kilometres. Depending on the season, it can support between 50,000 and 70,000 sheep.

The largest sheep move happened back in 1886, in Queensland. Some 27 horsemen moved about 43,000 sheep over a distance of 64 km from Barcaldine to Beaconsfield station.

Fastest Sheep Shearers

According to the 1993 *Guinness Book of Records*, Alan McDonald holds the record for the fastest speed of sheep shearing in a single working day. On 20 December 1990, at Waitnaguru, New Zealand, he machine-sheared 805 lambs in nine hours (about 40.2 seconds per lamb!).

The hand-shearing record is held by Peter Casserly, of Christchurch in New Zealand. On 13 February 1976, he cut the wool off 353 lambs in just nine hours.

The record for the number of sheep machine-shorn in a 24-hour period is 2200! This record is held by Alan McDonald and Keith Wilson. They did this massive task at Warkworth in New Zealand, on 26 January 1988. They may be fast, but it would still take them a long time to shear Australia's 180 million or so sheep!

fairly large animal that can weigh up to 100 kg and it can be uncooperative. Many injuries happen while just trying to manhandle the sheep into position. Also, the temperature in a shearing shed can reach 40°C, and this can lead to exhaustion and mistakes in shearing.

One system invented by the Merino Wool Harvesting Company gently but firmly grabs the sheep in its robot arms. There are a few shearing 'arms', which have sensors to allow the arms to move the shears close to the sheep's body without cutting its skin. The overall system is actually cheaper than getting humans to shear the wool and, apparently, the wool is free of blood.

CSIRO scientists are working on ways to remove the fleece without any shearing at all. They are experimenting with a hormone called Epidermal Growth Factor. This weakens the wool, so that after about five weeks you can come along and just pluck it off with your bare hands. The sheep is left with a short stubble to protect it from the weather. The sheep has an easier time losing its wool (no cuts or rough handling), and the wool is of a better quality, because all the fibres are the same length, and there are no short fibres from a 'second cut'.

It's taken a lot more than woolly thinking to get the fleece off the sheep's back!

Flight, Food & Thingummyjigs

Contents

The Utility

The world's first utility was invented in Australia in 1934 — and ended up as the bestselling car in America!

It was invented during the Great Depression in the 1930s. Money was very tight. The utility came into existence because of a farmer who could not afford both a car for his family and a truck for his farm. Banks would not lend money to farmers to buy a luxury like a car, but they would lend money to buy a working vehicle like a truck. So the farmer (or his wife — the history books differ on this point) wrote a letter to the managing director of the Ford Car Company:

Why don't you build people like me a vehicle in which I can take my family to church on Sunday, and my pigs to town on Monday?

The letter bounced around inside the Ford Company. It went from the Managing Director, to the Sales Department, to the Finance Department, to the Production Department, to the Chief Body Engineer, and finally to the Body Designer, Mr Lewis T. Bandt.

Lewis Bandt was an exceptional young man. His family were struggling farmers in South Australia. The family left farming and moved to Adelaide. Lewis was the eldest of five children. In 1924, Lewis started work as an apprentice fitter-and-turner with

Holden Invented the Ute — Not!

Sir Lawrence Hartnett of Holden also claimed that he invented the ute. He says that on a trip from Sydney to Melbourne he stopped in at Gundagai to see the local Holden dealer. The dealer was very unhappy. He had almost sold a Chevrolet passenger car to a farmer, but the bank would not lend money on what they thought was a luxury. As he drove out of Gundagai, he thought about this problem. Then the idea came to him in a flash: *make a coupe utility, with a snug all-metal cabin and a handy tray body at the back.* Soon he had utes pouring off the Holden production line.

His Holden ute came out a bit later than the Ford ute, and, like the Ford ute, it sold very well.

Death of the Utility — Not!

Australian-made utes had their maximum sales in the late 1960s and early 1970s. Back then, about 20,000 Holden utes were sold each year. But then the sales began to drop — petrol became very expensive, and the new Japanese imports with smaller engines were cheap to buy and cheap to run. By the mid-1980s, Holden and Valiant utes had vanished from the market.

But since then, petrol prices have stopped climbing and imported cars have become more expensive. So Australian-made utes with their bigger engines became more popular again. For the year of 1995, ute sales were 6000 for Holden and 7000 for Ford.

a company, Duncan & Fraser, that modified and sold Ford Model-T cars. He soon began to design body shapes for Duncan & Fraser. When he was 17, he moved to Melbourne to work with Melbourne Body Works. Around 1928, at the age of 18, he left to start work as a draughtsman with Ford at their newly built factory in Geelong.

Mr Bandt was only 22 years old when he started thinking about what a vehicle that could take a family to church on Sunday and the pigs to town on Monday would look like. When he put his final ideas down on paper, he realised that he had quite a handsome and well-balanced vehicle. He had married the front of a car with the back of a truck. It was called a *coupe utility* — *coupe*, because it was designed to carry two people, and *utility*, because the farmer could use the back section to carry anything.

Sure, there had been some light trucks and delivery vans made before this time — but usually they had only a half-door in the passenger compartment, and sometimes no door at all. And if there was a roof to the passenger compartment it was only a canvas roof. So the people in the front would get wet in the rain.

Often, there was not even a panel separating the passenger compartment from the back where the load was carried. This was very unsafe in an accident. There were even some handmade utilities, which had been carved up by an enthusiastic farmer with a saw, or even an axe! And the suspension in these vehicles was always very rough, because the vehicle had been designed to carry a heavy load.

This Australian-made utility was the first to offer a fully-sealed passenger compartment, made of metal. It was based on the front of the new Ford V-8 sedan. It had metal doors, a metal roof and windows made of glass. The cargo section, the side panels and the rear of the cab were all pressed from a single piece of metal. The cargo section was totally separate, and could be covered with a special piece of canvas. This was a great idea, especially if you were carrying a few hundred kilograms of smelly fertiliser or pig manure! And of course, the suspension had been specially designed to suit the car.

The classic 1934 ford ute

Japanese Car Imports to America

The Japanese car makers almost certainly knew how Americans love their utilities (or 'pick-ups'). In 1956, the very first Japanese cars brought into America were 16 small utilities. In 1966, 65,000 Japanese cars were imported into America – and by 1992, this had risen to 2,484,092.

By October 1933, Ford Australia had built two prototypes of the utility. Lewis Bandt asked a salesman if he could sell them easily. 'Heck,' said the salesman, 'give me 100 and I could sell them tomorrow.' The salesman was right. These coupe utilities rolled right off the production line in 1934 and straight onto farms. The banks would lend the farmers money to buy them, because they were a work vehicle — thanks to the back section, which could carry a load of half a tonne.

In 1935, Mr Bandt took two of his coupe utilities to America and showed them to Henry Ford, who had started the Ford Motor Company. In Australia we have always called such a vehicle a 'ute' or 'utility' — which means 'useful' or 'designed for many different, and often heavy-duty, practical uses'. But Henry Ford called the utility the 'kangaroo chaser'. In most of America it was called

Sunday...

Monday...

Ute on a Stamp

In February 1997, Australia Post issued four stamps that showed cars. The cars were the 1948 Holden FX, the 1958 Austin Lancer, the 1962 Chrysler Valiant R-Series, and the 1934 Ford Coupe Utility.

a 'pick-up truck' — because it was like a small truck, and they could pick up loads with it. The Texans called the utility a 'ranchero', because they used it on their ranches. The utility was an instant worldwide success.

Mr Bandt got the design right on his first production model. Every utility today is very similar to that original car, built in Ford's factory in Geelong, Victoria.

But the story of the ute has a sad end. Mr Bandt, well and healthy at the age of 80, died in the car that he invented. His fully restored 1933 Ford Coupe Utility had a number plate that read UT-001. The petrol gauge was a glass tube with a bubble inside. The 54-year-old speedometer looked like an ancient clock. It read 83,909 miles when he collided with a sand truck on 18 March 1987.

Lawrence Hargrave

Lawrence Hargrave walked on water! Although he wasn't the first person ever reported to do this, he was certainly the first Australian. He was also the first Australian to fly. In a machine made of four box kites, and held together with 24 rubber bands, he flew nearly 5 metres off the ground! Scientific papers all over the world wrote up this flight.

Hargrave was born in England on 29 January 1850. His parents left him at a boarding school and came to Australia when he was six. When he turned 15, he travelled to Australia.

argrave's father was a Judge of the Supreme Court of New South Wales. He wanted Lawrence to study law. However, Lawrence was not interested in law, and when he didn't pass the law exams his father let him go his own way.

He got an apprenticeship with the Australian Steam Navigation Company. There he learnt many important skills. By the time he left he knew how to make accurate drawings, as well as how to work wood and metal.

When Hargrave walked on water, it wasn't his religious beliefs that stopped him from sinking. Instead, the practical 20-year-old had built himself long, hollow, boat-shaped shoes! These had hinged flaps underneath to 'grip' the water as he moved his feet backward, and to fold up when he moved his feet forward. He often took short cuts straight across Rushcutters Bay in Sydney, from where he lived to where he worked.

After his apprenticeship, he spent the years between 1872 and 1877 travelling to, and across, Papua New Guinea. On one journey the boat *Maria* smashed to pieces on a Queensland reef. Thirty-five members of the crew died. This didn't stop him from joining another expedition. He navigated the *Neva* up the Fly River in Papua New Guinea and made the first navigation charts of the river.

Around 1878 he came back to Sydney, and worked at the Sydney Observatory until 1883 as an

Lawrence Hargrave Jnr. loved to ski behind his father's boat shoes.

Assistant Astronomical Observer to H.C. Russell. He married in 1878, and eventually had four daughters and a son. While working at the observatory, he observed the transit of Mercury across the face of the sun.

In 1883, a volcano called Krakatoa erupted. Krakatoa was a small volcanic island in Indonesia. It was one of the greatest explosions in recorded history — much bigger than the biggest nuclear

The French & Hargrave

The early French flyers always acknowledged their debt to Hargrave.

When Alberto Santos-Dumont made the first heavier-than-air flight in France in 1906, his plane had wings made with Hargrave box kites. And when Gabriel Voisin built the first aircraft that people could buy he called them 'Hargraves' because of the Hargrave box kites built into the wings.

weapon ever exploded. Even though it was thousands of kilometres away, the noise of the explosion was heard in Sydney!

This explosion was followed by amazingly beautiful sunsets. Hargrave put forward a theory that it was the volcanic dust in the upper atmosphere that was causing the stunning sunsets. The Royal Society in Britain formed a special committee to investigate the eruption. They chose Hargrave's theory of the dust causing the colourful sunsets as the best of all the theories they had read from around the world. (In recent times, scientists have begun to talk about the concept of a 'nuclear winter' — the cooling down of our planet after huge amounts of dust are thrown up by many nuclear explosions. These scientists are following on from Hargrave's original ideas about the effects of dust on the atmosphere.)

In 1883, Hargrave received some land from his father. The income from this land meant that he would never have to work again. In the future, he could spend his energy on anything he liked — and what he liked was flight.

Hargrave studied the way birds, fish, snakes and insects moved and he began building models of planes. His first designs had flapping wings — like a bird's. On 31 December 1884, he got his first model plane to fly. It weighed only 30 grams and had two flapping wings driven by stretched rubber bands. He continued to make models driven by rubber bands for the next four years. His best model had

Moving Air + Helmet = No Head

When air moves over a curved surface like a motorbike helmet, there is a lifting force on the helmet. The faster that the air moves, the greater the lifting force.

In fact, there are rumours that some United States Air Force pilots have actually had their heads pulled off when they have had to eject from their planes at supersonic speeds.

The Russians have known about this problem. They have given their pilots a helmet with a double skin – and the outer skin has holes drilled in it. These holes make the air flow over the helmet roughly and turbulently, not smoothly. The turbulent air has very little lift, and so pilots survive a high-speed ejection with their heads still joined to their shoulders!

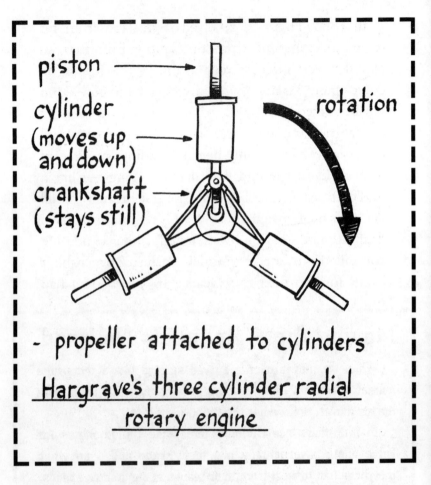

piston →

cylinder
(moves up
and down) →

crankshaft →
(stays still)

rotation

- propeller attached to cylinders

Hargrave's three cylinder radial
rotary engine

48 rubber bands and flapping wings and it flew 100 metres through the air!

For a while, he built flying machines with compressed air driving the wings. This principle is used in some of today's more advanced helicopters. But Hargrave soon realised that flapping wings were not the way to go.

In 1891, he got his first fixed-wing (not flapping wing), propeller-driven plane to fly. It was powered by a three-cylinder engine.

Hargrave needed more power to get a machine to fly higher and further, so he started working on other types of engines. He had just the skills needed: he was very creative and inventive, always coming up with new ideas, and he was a skilled draughtsman, so he could put his ideas down on paper. He was also skilled at many trades, so he could actually build the dreams he could see in his mind.

He realised that steam engines were just too heavy for a plane. Steam engines had to have a water supply, a furnace to heat the water, fuel to provide the heat, a boiler to store the pressure, and so on. But exactly what kind of engine would be the best for a flying machine?

Altogether he designed 52 engines, and built about 33 of them. They included horizontally opposed cylinder engines (like in Subaru and Volkswagen motor cars), single-cylinder engines (like many small motorbikes), rotary and semi-rotary engines (like Mazda Wankel car engines), jet-propeller engines, and a pure jet engine. To power these engines he tried steam, petrol, kerosene, carbonic acid and even gunpowder. And he had to build almost everything himself.

He was one of the few people in Australia who even believed it was possible to build flying machines. Most people laughed at the idea. In 1892, Hargrave wrote to a friend: *The people of Sydney who can speak of my work without a smile are scarce.* However, the friends who did not laugh at him and gave him their facilities and help included Mr H.C. Russell, Professor Threlfall, and Professor Pollock of the Physics Department of the University of Sydney.

In 1893 Hargrave moved to Stanwell Park, New South Wales. Here he started working out what kind of surfaces would best support weight. He started making box kites. They were not just small kites like the ones you take and fly in the park. The biggest one he made was 3 metres long, 1.5 metres high and nearly 4 metres wide. It was still very light, weighing only 11 kg. Hargrave's box kites played a big role in the design of the early European biplanes.

On 12 November 1894, he joined four of his box kites together and added a seat underneath to sit in. With a 34 kph wind blowing, he was lifted 4.6 metres into the air by one of his box kites, stayed there for a while, and returned safely to earth! This was an enormous achievement. In his paper to the Royal Society of New South Wales, he wrote: *A safe means of making an ascent with a flying machine ... and making a descent, are now at the service of any experimenter.*

In 1897 he made one of his greatest discoveries — one that has influenced practically every flying

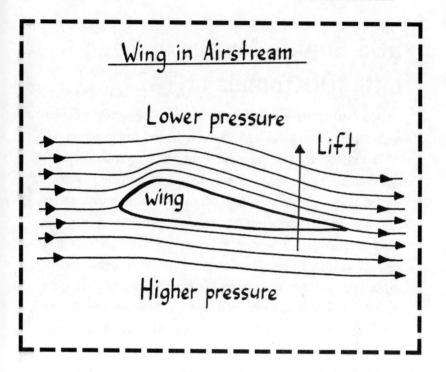

Wing in Airstream

Lower pressure

Lift

wing

Higher pressure

machine ever built. Most of his kites had flat surfaces. But he noticed that if air flowed over a surface that had the curved side up, there would be a lifting force. The air stream actually 'pulls' the curved surface up. He called his curved wing the 'aerocurve'.

Hargrave published his results and in 1898 Mr A.A. Merrill of the Boston Aeronautical Society copied Hargrave's work. In a paper published in the *Aeronautical Journal* in 1899, he described how well Hargrave's curved wings worked and how he had come up with an improved design that gave 14% more lift.

525 Square Metres of Wing Lift, 400 Tonnes of 747

How does an aeroplane fly? There are two popular explanations, which are both partly right and partly wrong.

The first is the Bernoulli (or Equal Transit Time) explanation. It says that the top surface of the wing is more curved that the bottom surface, so the air there moves faster and has lower pressure. The higher pressure under the wing then pushes the wing up. The first problem with this explanation is that stunt planes and supersonic fighters have wings with the same shape on the top and bottom – how do they fly? The second problem is that the distance over the top of the wing on a typical small plane would have to be about 50% longer than the distance under the wing. A Cessna 172 wing has a top surface that is about 2% longer than the bottom surface – according to this theory it would have to reach about 650 kph just to get airborne! So how does a Cessna 172 fly? A final problem with this explanation is that it ignores the aerodynamics on the bottom surface of the wing.

The second popular explanation is the Newtonian (or Angle of Attack) explanation. It says that the front of the wing is higher than the back of the wing. The air hits the bottom of the wing and is pushed downwards – and in reaction, the wing is pushed upwards. One problem with this explanation is that at speeds under 5000 kph, the air doesn't actually hit the wing – it normally gets deflected away. Another problem is that this explanation completely ignores the top of the wing, which contributes a lot to the lift.

There is also the Mathematical Aerodynamics description, which uses complicated university-level maths and computer simulations. It takes account of the shapes of the top and the bottom of the wing, and the angle of attack of the wing — and you'd need a maths degree to understand it.

In fact, the Wright brothers, who, in 1903, were the first people to fly in a powered aeroplane, used curved surfaces for the wings of their planes.

Three years earlier, in 1900, the Wright brothers had written to the aerial navigator Octave Chanute, asking him to give them a list of books and papers so they could learn what work others had done in the field of flying. Chanute replied on 17 May 1900: *You will find accounts in the* Aeronautical Journals *of April 1898 [Hargrave's Royal Society paper, 'Soaring in a Horizontal Wind'] and July 1899 [Merrill's tests on Hargrave's aerocurve] …*

Hargrave continued his work, now paying special attention to new types of fuel. He was always considering ways to make things lighter — something few other inventors were worrying about.

Hargrave did all his work alone. He did not get support from any scientific, financial or government body in Australia. Because information took so long

The Radial Rotary Engine

Another great invention of Hargrave's was the radial rotary engine. He developed this around February 1889. It's a good example of just how lateral a thinker he was.

In an engine, there's a piston inside each cylinder. Each piston moves up and down, and gives a little 'push' to the crankshaft and makes the crankshaft spin around. Modern engines have four, six or even eight pistons. With so many little 'pushes' the crankshaft spins quite smoothly. In Hargrave's day, engines had only one, two or three cylinders. The crankshaft didn't spin smoothly, but in a bumpy way.

So engines had a wheel built into them to smooth out the bumps. The disadvantage of this wheel was that it was very heavy – and you didn't need extra weight in a flying machine.

Hargrave's brilliant idea was to think backwards. Instead of keeping the cylinders still and spinning the crankshaft, he kept the crankshaft still and spun the cylinders around *it*!

The propeller was attached to the cylinders. The cylinders were quite heavy, and made the turning motion smooth.

His invention of the radial rotary engine was published in *Transactions of The Royal Society* in 1889. Thirty-three copies of this publication were sent to France.

The French built the Gnome radial rotary engine. It was the most important engine in the early days of flying. It appeared in 1909, and was *the* engine to use in aeroplanes for some 20 years.

to reach Australia he often repeated work that had already been done overseas. His work, however, was published in many international journals. Hargrave never took a patent out on any of his inventions, because he thought everyone should have access to information!

Unfortunately, he made one major mistake. In all his years of work he did not realise that he should improve the efficiency of the propellers on his planes. For instance, he didn't try changing the pitch of the propeller — the angle at which it cuts into the air. The propellers for one of his full-size planes built in 1902 had a maximum efficiency of 17%. But at the same time other inventors were building propellers with an efficiency of 70%. That meant that they could use a less powerful (and therefore lighter) engine to pull the plane just as hard through the air.

Although it had long been his dream to be the first to fly, when the Wright brothers beat him to it Hargrave immediately wrote to congratulate them.

The plane he designed in 1902 actually did get to fly — but 90 years later! In 1992, students from the University of Sydney rebuilt his 1902 plane from the original plans. They used a modern engine instead of his underpowered engine — and his plane flew!

Around 1910, Hargrave offered his 170 or so models and designs to the University of Sydney (although some books say that it was to Sydney's Technological Museum, now the Powerhouse Museum) to store and display. However, they could not come up with the £300 needed to buy display cases for them. The only museum that would agree to his conditions was the Deutsches Technological Museum in Munich, Germany — so they got his collection! During World War II, all but around 23 of these models and designs were destroyed in a bomb attack. The West German Government presented these 'survivors' as a gift to Sydney in 1960, and they are now stored at the Powerhouse Museum.

Hargrave died in 1915, only two months after his only son, Geoffrey, was killed at Gallipoli. He dearly loved his son, who had helped him build planes and engines. Hargrave died of complications from an operation, but romantics like to believe that it was the same bullet that killed both father and son.

Octave Chanute, Chicago engineer and aerial navigator, wrote this: *If there is one man more than another who deserves to fly through the air, that man is Lawrence Hargrave of Sydney, New South Wales.*

In 1910, Alexander Graham Bell, the inventor of the telephone, visited Sydney. He was very keen to meet Hargrave, with whom he had often exchanged letters. At an address that Bell gave at the University of Sydney, Bell said: 'Mr Lawrence Hargrave is known better in America than in his own country.

In America, we regard him as standing on the same pinnacle as [Samuel] Langley, [Sir Hiram] Maxim and Chanute. Indeed, his work formed the basis of our modern progress and teaching regarding the navigation of the air.

'The first ... aeroplanes were modelled direct upon the Hargrave box kite, and wherever we have departed from the stable model, we have had to substitute skill for automatic stability in the air. Heavy mortality has been the result of our disregard for the very stable form that Mr Hargrave has given to the world in the box kite.'

Lawrence was a generous and clever man who gave his ideas freely to the world. He contributed greatly to the science of flight, and came close to being the first to fly. He is remembered by a memorial at Stanwell Park, and the Lawrence Hargrave Chair of Aeronautical Engineering at the University of Sydney.

Australian Crawl

Postcard pictures of Australia are full of sun and water. And no wonder — our wonderful climate and beaches have combined to produce more than their fair share of swimming stars for Australia. In fact, of the 68 Olympic gold medals won by Australia between 1896 and 2000, 46 were gained in swimming events. Most of those 46 gold medals were won in the freestyle event, which is swum using the Australian crawl.

We humans are practically the only land animal that does not know instinctively how to swim. The other land animals swim simply by doing a modified version of their ordinary walk — so a dog swims using the 'dog paddle'. But we humans have always had to be taught how to swim.

It was 4500 years ago that an unknown Egyptian made a hieroglyph for swimming.

Over 2000 years ago, the Greeks and the Romans were taught how to swim as a part of their training to be soldiers. The Romans had swimming pools that were quite separate from their baths. It is thought that Gaius Maecenas built the first heated swimming pool in the first century BC. In Japan around the first century BC they had swimming races and this tradition lasted so long that swimming training was compulsory in Japanese schools until the 17th century.

Most Famous Swimming Pool in the World

The Olympic Swimming Pool at North Sydney, just next to the Sydney Harbour Bridge, is famous for being the pool where the highest number of world records was set. It was here that 86 world swimming records were set between 1955 and 1978.

By 1500, swimming had become very unpopular in Europe. People thought that you could get a disease from the water by swimming in it.

But gradually, swimming regained its popularity. In 1810, Lord Byron swam the Dardanelles to show that Leander, a mythological character, could have swum it on his nightly visits to his beloved, the priestess Hero. (The Dardanelles were navigated to put soldiers ashore at Gallipoli — see the story 'Escape from Gallipoli' in *Ears, Gears & Gadgets*.) By the 1840s there were organised swimming races in England.

In 1873, Mr J. Arthur Trudgen introduced into England a swimming style that had an overarm stroke, similar to what became known as the Australian crawl. However, the Trudgen overarm stroke was quite slow, because the leg kick involved bringing the knee up as far as the hips. Lifting the knee up that far created a lot of resistance in the water and slowed you down.

The first ever recorded swimming championship was a 440-yard (402.3-metre) race at Woolloomooloo Bay in Sydney on 14 February 1846. The first World Swimming Championship was held in Melbourne on 9 January 1858. This was at the time of the Victorian gold rush, when people from all over the world were

Largest Swimming Pools

According to the 1993 *Guinness Book of Records*, the largest sea-water swimming pool in the world is the Orthlieb in Casablanca, Morocco. It is 480 metres by 75 metres and covers an area of 3.6 hectares.

The largest landlocked swimming pool in the world is Willow Lake in Warren, Ohio. It's 183 metres by 46 metres.

Australian Prime Minister Drowned

On 17 December 1967, the Australian Prime Minister, Harold Holt, drowned while swimming in wild surf at Portsea in Victoria. There were even some rumours that he was taken onto a Chinese submarine!

recklessly throwing away their money in the hope of striking a fortune in gold. More than 1000 people came to watch Joe Bennett of Sydney win the race and become the first world champion swimmer.

But it was after this that we invented our own swimming style — the Australian crawl! It's typical of a lot of history that nobody is really sure who invented it or how it got its name.

It's *almost* certain that the Australian crawl came from the South Pacific, via a young Solomon Islander, Alick Wickham. Alick, the son of a European trader and a woman from the Solomon Islands, came to Australia around 1898, aged 10, for his education. It's said that his swimming coach, George Farmer, was so amazed watching him in a swimming race at Bronte in Sydney that he yelled out: 'Look at that boy crawling over the water!' Soon Farmer was teaching others this strange new style.

Anyhow, that's one version of how the Australian crawl got its name.

It is fairly certain that Arthur Cavill changed and improved the Australian crawl. Cavill was born in London, but came to Australia with his family in

1879. At the age of 21, Arthur Cavill held the Australian swimming title for 220 yards (roughly 200 metres). His whole family was involved in swimming. They all participated in both races and coaching. Apparently, Cavill actually saw Alick Wickham training. He realised what a great style it was and started using it in races himself. Arthur Cavill stopped using the Trudgen kick, and began using the flutter kick (the legs 'flutter' up and down from the hips).

The other version of how the Australian crawl got its name relates to Cavill's amazing swimming ability. An angry competitor said that that he wasn't going to let 'Cavill crawl all over' him — hence the name, Australian crawl.

Olympic Seconds

If our swimmers want an advantage at the next Olympics they might want to grow their fingernails! At least, this is what John Chapman of Western Australia claimed in a letter to the *New Scientist* of 31 August 1996.

Today, swimming times are being measured down to 0.001 seconds. For a fast swimmer covering 100 metres, this corresponds to a distance of 1 mm. A long fingernail might mean the difference between a gold and a silver medal!

Swimming Styles

There are now five main recognised swimming strokes. They are the breaststroke (probably the oldest style of swimming), the sidestroke, the butterfly (developed by the American Henry Myers in 1933), the backstroke (first used by the American Harry Hebner at the 1912 Olympic Games) and the Australian crawl.

There is no Olympic event that specifically features the Australian crawl. However, in the freestyle swimming event, the swimmer is free to choose any swimming style that they like. They all choose the Australian crawl, because it's the fastest.

Cavill ended up working as a swimming coach in America. He introduced the Australian crawl to the rest of the world.

Duke Kahanamoku, the Hawaiian swimmer who won three Olympic gold medals (in 1912 and 1920), helped improve the Australian crawl. He addded more flutter kicks — six per arm stroke cycle, not two. (He was also the Sheriff of Honolulu from 1932 to 1961 and was paid to officially greet famous visitors to Honolulu.) Australian swimmers started using his style of flutter kick after his Australian visit of 1914 to 1915.

The Australian crawl has been modified since then. But it is certainly the basis of the swimming style used in all freestyle events ever since!

Australian Flag

How old do you reckon the inventor of the Australian flag was? Maybe 50, maybe 39, or how about 93? No way! Ivor Evans was only 14 years old when his flag design was picked as a winner in 1901! (Actually, he shared the prize money with four other people who had entered identical designs.)

His flag design came first in a competition organised by the Commowealth Government. Over 32,823 designs were submitted for the competition — but Ivor's design won.

We've all seen the current Australian flag. It has a navy blue background. The Union Jack is in the top left corner, while the Southern Cross fills up the right of the flag. Directly under the Union Jack is a seven-pointed star. Six of those points stand for a state, while the seventh point represents the Commonwealth of Australia. (The seventh point was added in 1909 to represent the Commonwealth of Australia, or the Northern Territory, or all the Territories of the Commonwealth of Australia, or Papua — depending on which history book you read!)

But this wasn't the first flag ever flown in Australia.

Our first flag was the Union Flag, which was first raised by Captain James Cook at Stingray Harbour (later called Botany Bay), on 29 April 1770.

The Union Flag is different from the Union Jack. The Union Flag was made by combining the Cross of St George (patron saint of England) with the Cross of St Andrew (patron saint of Scotland). In 1801, the Cross of St Patrick (patron saint of Ireland) was added to the Union Flag, making it the Union Jack.

Captain Arthur Phillip also flew a Union Flag when he landed in Sydney Harbour. A Union Flag is flown every day on a flagpole in Loftus Street, Sydney, near where Phillip landed.

Our second flag, and the very first all-Australian flag, was made in 1806. Mrs Honor Bowman cut up her beautiful wedding dress to make a flag to fly at

Flags as Symbols

A flag is usually a piece of coloured cloth that acts as a symbol for a group of people. These people can be members of a state, a government department, a branch of the Armed Forces, or even a sports club.

A flag usually has simple patterns, and uses only six main colours, to make it easy to see and recognise — red, white, blue, green, yellow and black.

The word flag appears in common sayings in our language. To 'win the flag/pennant' means to win a competition; to 'show the flag' means to show your strength, without actually using it; to 'run it up the flagpole and see who salutes' means to make an idea or suggestion and see how much support there is for it; to 'strike the flag' means to surrender.

In past times, the black flag was the symbol of pirates. The white flag means 'truce' or 'surrender', while the red flag means 'revolution' or 'mutiny'. The yellow flag means 'infectious diseases, beware'. In the days before modern medicine, it would be carried by a ship to warn others that it had people on board infected with a disease such as yellow fever, or cholera.

her home in Richmond, New South Wales. Her flag was rich in detail. It had an emblem shaped like a shield in the centre. On one side of the emblem was a kangaroo and on the other side was an emu — just

Biggest Flags

The biggest flag in regular use is the flag of Brazil — 70 metres by 100 metres. But the biggest flag ever made measures 78 metres by 154 metres, and weighs 1.38 tonnes. This American 'Superflag' was made by Humphrey's Flag Company of Pottstown, Pennsylvania.

like on the Australian Coat of Arms. This original flag is now in the Mitchell Library in Sydney.

Our third flag was never very popular — even though the Lords of the Admiralty gave the 'National Colonial Flag for Australia' their official approval. This flag was designed in the early 1820s by two ships' captains — John Nicholson and John Bingle. Not one of these flags has survived, but we do know that it had the red Cross of St George, with a star in each corner to symbolise the Southern Cross. (Maybe it never became popular because of complaints from Scottish and Irish people whose national flags had been left out!)

The fourth Australian flag appeared in 1851. It was the flag of the Australian Anti-transportation Society. The Australian Anti-transportation Society wanted to stop the transportation of convicts from Britain to the eastern colonies of what would later be called Australia. The British Government wouldn't agree to this, but on 1 February 1851 they did stop transportation to New South Wales and the Moreton Bay District (now part of Queensland).

The Society's flag had the Union Jack and the five stars of the Southern Cross. The stars represented New South Wales (which at that time included Queensland), South Australia, Tasmania, Victoria and New Zealand. (Western Australia wasn't counted, because only a handful of non-Aborigines lived there at that time.) An official party of the Anti-transportation Society took this flag to England and back again.

In the early 1850s, the *Swordfish* was the first trading ship to carry the flag of the Anti-transportation Society. It was sailing under the command of Captain John Clinch on a river inlet in Hobart. Captain J.H. Gennys of the British ship *Fantome* was passing by. He didn't recognise the new flag and demanded that this strange flag be taken down.

Captain Clinch shouted back angrily: 'That's the Australian flag — the Southern Cross — the symbol of freedom! And it's about time we had our own flag, too!'

Captain Gennys was not impressed. 'Indeed! You know as well as I do there's no Australian flag. Haul it down at once, sir, or I'll do so myself!'

'Aye, you've got the advantage of me — I'll haul it down myself,' replied Captain Clinch. 'But mark you

The Aussie flag ... complete with sauce stain!

Flap

this! There'll come a day when the Australian flag will be known in all the seven seas. Aye, known and respected! But hauled down — never! For no man!'

Captain Clinch was angry at being forced to take the flag down and scornfully hoisted a tablecloth up onto the mast. He wanted to show the British ship that he would fly *anything* rather than a British flag!

You can see a good specimen of the Society's flag in the Queen Victoria Museum in Launceston, Tasmania.

Our fifth flag was flown at the Eureka Stockade on 3 December 1854. It also used the Southern Cross as a symbol of freedom. It has a white cross with broad stripes on a blue background. Four of the five stars of the Southern Cross are located on each of the four ends of the cross, while the fifth star is in the centre of the cross. You can see the remains of this original flag, some 3.6 metres by 2.4 metres, in the Ballarat Art Gallery.

Oldest Flag

We don't know who first used flags, but they must have been used for a long time. Flags are useful in a battle to identify the commander and to send messages. Early civilisations in the Middle East, China, Egypt and India all used flags.

According to the 1993 *Guinness Book of Records*, the oldest flag we know of was used some 5000 years ago (around 3000 B.C.) in what is now Iran. This metal flag was discovered in 1972. It's quite small — only 23 square centimetres. It shows an eagle, a bull, a goddess, two lions and three women.

Chinese records tell us that the founder of the Chou Dynasty (around 1122 B.C.) would always have a white flag carried in front of him.

The Bible makes many references to banners and standards. Isaiah 11:12 says: *He will raise a banner for the nations and gather the exiles of Israel; he will assemble the scattered people of Judah from the four quarters of the earth.* Numbers 2:2 says: *The Israelites are to camp around the Tent of Meeting some distance from it, each man under his standard with the banners of his family.*

The Eureka Stockade was a crude fort built in Ballarat, Victoria. It was there that a bitter struggle took place between miners, soldiers and police.

The miners were rebelling against the enormously high licence fee they had to pay. If they didn't have a licence they weren't allowed to dig for gold, and they still had to pay the licence fee even if they didn't find any gold. There was a special group of armed police

Flags Change with Time

The flag of what would eventually be called Libya first appeared in 1947. The black flag, with a central crescent and white star, was actually the flag of the Sanusi religious sect. Libya was first called Cyrenaica. In 1951, Fezzan and Tripolitania joined to form the country called Libya, and so stripes of red and green were added to symbolise these countries.

In 1969, the monarchy was overthrown in a revolution, and the flag was changed again to three of the Arab colours — red, white and black. In 1971, Libya joined with Syria and Egypt to form the Confederation of Arab Republics — and so the Confederation's emblem, a gold hawk, was added to the centre stripe.

But by 1977, Libya was angered by the decision of Egypt to make peace with Israel, and showed its anger by changing its flag again. The flag is now just plain green, the fourth Islamic colour.

that made the licence checks. The miners were also fighting against the brutal, corrupt officials.

One miner, James Scobie, was killed in Ballarat near the Eureka Hotel. But the official who killed him was charged only with manslaughter.

The situation became intolerable for the miners. About 500 of them, led by Peter Lalor, burnt their licences. Then they claimed Victoria as a Republic. The miners in the Eureka Stockade were ready to fight. This was Australia's first and, so far, only revolution, but the fighting lasted only 10 minutes! The authorities were cunning. Early in the morning, when there were only 150 miners in the stockade, nearly 300 policemen and soldiers turned up to fight. The miners, outnumbered two to one, were quickly overcome.

In the battle, six soldiers and about 22 miners were killed. The miners lost this battle, but they eventually won the war. In 1855 they got what they were fighting for — the licence fee was abolished.

Peter Lalor was wounded in the left arm during the battle. He escaped, but soon afterwards his arm had to be cut off at the shoulder. (This wouldn't happen today, with access to surgery and antibiotics.) A reward of £200 was offered for his capture. But public feeling was all in favour of the miners. Because of this, no miner was ever convicted, and an amnesty was later offered to everybody involved in the Eureka Stockade.

The Stars and Stripes

The Stars and Stripes flag of America is famous for its connection to a powerful sense of patriotism. The Congress resolved on 14 June 1777 that: *the Flag of the United States be 13 stripes, alternate red and white, that the Union be 13 stars, white in a blue field, representing a new constellation.* At that time, there were 13 states in the United States. But historians have never been able to find the original *Flag Law*, which would have given clear instructions about its design, and how and when to use it.

Each time a new state joined the United States, a new star was added to the flag. As a result, there have been 27 official American flags. The last change was in 1960, when the 50th state, Hawaii, was admitted. This new flag was first flown at one minute past midnight on 4 July 1960, at Fort McHenry National Monument in Baltimore, Maryland.

But the odd thing about such a famous flag is its early history – we don't know who designed it, who made the first Stars and Stripes, or even if it ever flew in any battle of the American Revolution! It was only in 1783, well after the Revolutionary War was over, that George Washington actually got hold of a Stars and Stripes flag.

Meanwhile, people had got some money together to buy Lalor 60 hectares of land near Ballarat. Because he owned this land, he could now enter

Parliament. (In those days, only people who owned property could enter Parliament.) In 1855 he was elected for the seat of Ballarat. He stayed in Parliament for 27 years. During this period he held the positions of Postmaster-General, Minister of Trade and Customs, and even Speaker of the House.

The sixth Australian flag, our current one, began with a competition carried out by a newspaper, the Melbourne *Herald*. In 1900, Australia was about to change from a bunch of colonies of Great Britain to a separate country called Australia — but it didn't

Flag of Convenience

The naval phrase 'flag of convenience' means that a ship belonging to one country is registered under the flag of another country. The advantage of a 'flag of convenience' to the ship owners is that they don't have to follow the rules of their native country. For example, they can pay lower wages to the sailors, avoid paying some taxes, and choose not to follow some safety regulations. This is good for the ship owner, but generally bad for the sailors.

Liberia and Panama are both poor countries – but they are the main countries in which ships of other nations are registered. In fact, in 1992, Liberia officially had the biggest merchant fleet in the world – with a total tonnage of over 55 million tonnes!

Flag of Truce

The 'flag of truce' is a white flag. If the truce flag is shown during a battle, it shows that the holders of the flag want to talk to their enemies, or surrender. Anybody holding such a flag cannot carry weapons, and cannot be attacked or captured.

have a flag. It was a newspaper, not the government, that ran a competition for a national flag! Of course, this competition had no official standing.

The competition was won by a Melbourne bookseller, Mr F. Thompson. His design was very busy — not only did it have the Union Jack and the Southern Cross, it also had six red stripes — standing for the six states of Australia.

Soon afterwards, another paper, *Review of Reviews*, carried out another competition for the Australian flag. This competition was still in progress when Australia was proclaimed a nation on New Year's Day, 1901.

So Australia became a nation without even having its own flag!

At this stage, the Australian Government decided to join in with the *Review of Reviews* competition for an Australian flag. The prize money was £75 from the paper, £75 from the Australian Government, and £50 from the Havelock Tobacco Company — a total of £200. Some 32,823 designs were sent in from all over the world.

There was not a lot of freedom in the choice of design. In the rules of the competition, the first condition insisted that the new flag *should be based on the British ensign, as in the flags of countries added to its folds, signalling to the beholder that it is an Imperial Union ensign of the British Empire.*

Five people submitted the same winning design — Ivor Evans and Egbert John Nuttall from Melbourne, Leslie John Hawkins from Sydney, Annie Dorrington from Perth, and William Stevens from Auckland, New Zealand. This flag was first flown over the Exhibition Building in Melbourne in 1901.

The design was approved in 1903 by King Edward VII. But it was officially adopted as the Australian flag only as recently as 1953, when Parliament passed the *Flags Act*.

The Southern Cross

The Southern Cross is a constellation of five bright stars, which are best seen from the Southern Hemisphere. It has been known about for thousands of years, but the Southern Cross was first written about by Augustine Royer only as recently as 1679.

The Southern Cross is on the flags of Australia, New Zealand and Western Samoa.

Australian or Austrian Flag?

One unfortunate person who badly needed an Australian flag was Mr E.H. Flack. Mr Flack was the *only* person competing for Australia in the 1896 Olympic Games, which were held in Athens. At this time Australia was not even called Australia – it was still a collection of colonies.

He won both the 800 metres and 1500 metres races. But there was no Australian flag to raise in his honour. At the presentation ceremony officials did what they could and hauled up an Austrian flag instead!

There is still a lot of debate over whether Australia needs a new flag. There seem to be two main issues.

One issue is the debate about whether Australia should become a republic and cut its legal and political ties with Great Britain. Some people say that Australia should have a brand new flag if it becomes a republic. But other people say that we should keep our links with the past, and they quote the example of the flag of Hawaii. Even though Hawaii is now a state of the United States of America, it still has the Union Jack taking up one quarter of its flag.

The other issue is whether we should acknowledge the original settlers of Australia, the

Aborigines. Some people say we should remove the Union Jack from the Australian flag, and replace it with the Aboriginal flag — which has the bottom half red (for the red earth of Australia, and for all the blood that has been shed in Australia), the top half

One Nation, Many Flags

The national flag of a nation stands for the people. But some nations have a state or government flag, to stand for the government. This government flag, if it's different from the national flag, will be flown over government buildings and over embassies in foreign lands. There are different flags again for ships — the merchant flag for merchant ships, and the ensign for government ships.

black (for the Aborigines), and a yellow circle in the middle (for the sun, which gives us life and that unites the people to the land).

If we get a new flag, maybe another kid will design it.

Natural Australian Foods

The members of the First Fleet made it safely to Sydney, halfway around the world. But only 18 months after they had arrived in 1788 they were beginning to run out of food.

The situation was so desperate that the flagship of the First Fleet, the 512-tonne *Sirius*, was sent to the Cape of Good Hope to collect grain. It returned in May 1789, but didn't bring back enough. The food supply was so low that by November 1789 food rations had to be cut.

The *Guardian,* another food supply ship, was on its way to Sydney, but unluckily it smashed on an iceberg near the Cape of Good Hope on 23 December 1789. By February 1790 there was so little food that Governor Phillip sent the *Sirius* to Norfolk Island to pick up supplies. Unfortunately, the *Sirius* was wrecked on a reef just off Norfolk Island on 19 March 1790.

The colony suffered a severe famine until the Dutch ship *Waaksamheydt* arrived nearly nine months later on 17 December 1790.

The First Fleeters were starving in the midst of plenty — there was bush food all around them, but they could not see it! While they were starving to death, the Aborigines ate very well, just as they had for thousands of years. They ate kangaroos, wallabies, echidnas, turtles and all types of birds — ducks, pigeons, snipes, quails, bustards and geese. They ate yams, seeds, berries, roots and wild honey. The seed of the acacia was made into a paste for food. They even made flour and bread from different grains.

The problem was that the Europeans weren't used to these plants and animals, so they simply couldn't see them as foods. In 1788, Captain Phillip was even heard to complain that the Aboriginal diet was very monotonous and lacked variety.

The First Fleeters had brought some animals for food, such as rabbits, to this new land, but these destroyed the local environments, and ultimately killed the local animals. The Europeans did not even try to learn about the local food sources. They preferred to live off dried or salted meat, sugar, flour, salt and tea, and their own plant foods.

Some parts of Australia are more fertile than other parts, so local tribes collected food in different ways. The nomadic desert Aborigines covered huge distances in their search for food. They would shift their camp as often as once every 10 days. The tribe

Bush Food

Vic Cherikoff is one person who has changed the way that many non-Aboriginal Australians think about bush food. Today, as a result of his work, in some Sydney cafes you can drink a 'wattlecino' instead of a 'cappuccino'!

In 1983, he realised that many of the traditional foods that the Aborigines used were not only good food with good nutrition in them, they also were a more environmentally friendly way to get food out of the Australian soil. At first, it was hard to convince people. So he set up food festivals, and offered people relatively unfamiliar foods such as witchetty grubs, wattleseed, warrigal greens and riberries.

Today, these rediscovered foods are becoming more popular, and even an airline now carries Vic's bush foods.

would forage in groups of 20 or so, and would cover some 2500 square kilometres. Each walk could be up to 550 km long. They knew of some 80 different plants and animals that were good eating. Their basic food was about 1.5 kg of wild tomatoes per person per day.

But they did not have to spend all their time looking for food. Groups of women spent about two hours of each day in all collecting food from plants, and catching small game such as rodents, birds and goannas.

The men would hunt larger animals such as kangaroos — a much more chancy business. For cooking, kangaroos would be gutted, and then usually put into a shallow pit, dug into hot coals. Snakes would be grilled whole, either stretched out over a fire or on hot coals. Goannas were often cooked in the same way as snakes, but could also be put on a skewer and mounted above the fire for faster, more even, cooking. The tail and the underbelly were the favourite portions.

Their diet helped to protect Aborigines from diabetes. If you have diabetes, too much sugar circulates in your bloodstream. If you have high sugar levels in the blood for 20 or more years, you are likely to suffer blindness, leg ulcers and amputations, and even kidney disease.

In Australia today, diabetes affects 20% of Aborigines, but only 3% of non-Aboriginal Australians. The main reason for this is that the types of food that Aborigines eat have changed. Scientists have found that traditional Aboriginal foods put sugar into the bloodstream much more slowly, and so are less likely to cause diabetes. Even non-Aboriginal diabetics would be helped by a traditional Aboriginal diet.

There are hundreds of seeds, roots and nuts that you can eat that come from native Australian plants. But at least 15 of them are poisonous.

The cycad palm grows in northern Australia, and along the eastern and southwestern coasts. It has a whole bunch of little nuts that grow above the leaves. The nuts are about 1 cm in diameter. The Aborigines would crack open the hard shell to get at the soft seed inside. The trouble is that about 1% of the weight of the soft seed is a deadly poison called cycasin. Even one small dose can give you cancer in your gut.

They still wanted to eat the seed, so they worked out a few ways to avoid getting poisoned.

One way was to crush the seed and leave it in fresh running water for a week. Then they would take it out of the water and grind it into a paste. Finally, they would wrap the paste in paperbark and roast it in hot ashes for a few hours.

Another way to get rid of the poison was to roll the seeds in hot sand and leave them out in the sun for a few days. Then they did the fresh running water trick again.

Both of these methods were really good at getting rid of the poison. But the Aborigines had another method that was even better — they would 'smell' which of the cycad seeds had no poison in them.

The nuts would fall off the palm tree when they were ripe. Once they had been lying on the ground for about a year, the poison would break down and no longer be dangerous. The Aborigines would gather a whole bunch of nuts that had been lying on the ground under the tree. Some would have been there for a few days, while some would have been there for more than a year. They would crack open the hard shell and look at the seeds very carefully, smelling them and crumbling them between their fingers. Somehow, the Aborigines could tell the difference between poisonous and safe seeds, even when they were blindfolded.

Scientists from La Trobe University lived with the Aborigines to try to learn their secret. They had to use expensive and complicated technology to get the same results that the Aborigines got with their noses. The scientists used a gas chromatograph — an electronic 'nose'. It would 'sniff' the tiny traces of gas and vapour that were coming from the seed.

The European colonists just did not appreciate the vast food resources of Australia. They foolishly tried to use European animals and plants.

The first new Australian food, the Granny Smith apple, appeared around 1868. The Granny Smith is a wonderful apple — it's very good to eat, it's one of the best cooking apples, and it keeps better in storage than practically any other apple. In the early days, the growers found that if they wrapped the apples in oiled tissue paper they could be successfully stored in cold storage for eight months. The Granny Smith apple was one of the first foods to be sent overseas in the chilling rooms of ships in the late 1800s. (You can read about the history of refrigeration in the stories 'Waterbag and Coolgardie Safe' and 'Refrigeration' in *Ears, Gears & Gadgets*.)

Granny Smith was actually born Maria Ann Sherwood, in 1800 in Sussex. She and her husband arrived in New South Wales in 1837. They ended up farming some land in Ryde, with their five children. By the time she was in her 60s, people called her 'Granny' because she always wore a quaint bonnet and an apron and carried an old-fashioned, two-lidded basket, and she did have grandchildren. Because her husband was handicapped, she always took their produce to and from the markets for him. In fact, she was the first female fruit agent in Sydney, and possibly Australia.

There are two quite different stories about the start of the famous Granny Smith apple.

The first story goes like this: in the mid-1860s Maria brought home some cases of apples from the Sydney Fruit Markets. Some of the apples were rotten. (Some people claim that these were

The good old Granny smith...

Tasmanian crabapples.) She threw them out on the bank of a creek that ran near her house. The story is that one of these rotting apples took root and grew into an apple tree, probably around 1868. A small 12-year-old boy, the son of a Mr E.H. Small, tasted one of the apples. Even though it was green, he said that it tasted better than any apple that he had ever tried. Anyway, that was the story that the boy gave in 1924.

The second story was told by her grandson, Benjamin Spurway, in 1956. He says that Granny Smith was given some apples by a fruit agent, to see how well they would cook. She made apple

Fish Traps

If you have a river or a stream nearby, an easy way to catch fish is to build fish traps. The Ngemba fish traps, near Brewarinna in New South Wales, are built at the junction of the Barwon and Darling Rivers. This enormous arrangement of rock walls is cleverly designed, with pens of various shapes and heights. This means that, for example, tiny fish will be able to escape from a pen with holes between the rocks, but the bigger fish will be trapped. If some fish prefer to stay near the bottom, you can catch them easily from a types of pen with fairly low rock walls. These different types of pen mean that different fish can be caught at different times of the year.

The Aborigines of the area would gather at these fish traps at different times of the year and could always be sure that there would be enough fish for a feast.

Unfortunately, much of the magnificent Ngemba fish traps has gradually been destroyed.

pies out of the apples. She threw the apple cores, with the seeds in them, out of her kitchen window. A few years later, the magic seedling was growing next to the kitchen wall.

Whichever story is true, Granny Smith used her skills as an orchardist to set up a whole orchard of these apples. She grafted small slivers of this strange new tree to other trees already growing. The orchard was in what is now the Sydney suburb of

Eastwood. She took the fruit to market in cases that were marked 'From Granny Smith's'.

The strange green apple was an instant success. It has earnt more money for Australian apple growers than all other types of apple combined. In fact, in 1975, 40% of all the apples grown in Australia and 50% of all the apples exported from Australia were Granny Smiths.

Unfortunately, when the orchard was subdivided for housing, that original tree was chopped down, dug out and burnt. Granny Smith died on 9 March 1870, aged 70. She has two memorials — a tombstone in St Anne's Church at Ryde, and millions of Granny Smith apple trees all over the world.

About 20% of Australia could be used to grow crops, but only 2% is actually cultivated. Perhaps we could use that other 18% to grow native foods.

Australian-made Foods

Some Australian foods — like Vegemite or the pavlova — are very artificial and look like nothing that you would find in nature. But there are plenty of dishes using fantastic fresh fruit and vegetables that bring together lots of different cooking styles.

There was one early attempt to set up a national style of food. The first Australian cookery book to use native foods was published in 1864. It was called *The English and Australian Cookery Book: Cookery for the Many as Well as the 'Upper Ten Thousand'*. It was written by Edward Abbott, who used the nom de plume 'An Australian Aristologist'. 'Aristologist' was a word invented in England in 1835 to mean 'one who is a student of the art of dining'. It comes from the Greek word for dinner — *ariston*. Abbott suggested eating Australian foods such as turtle soup and roast kangaroo. At the time, his ideas fell on deaf ears, but today a first edition of his book can fetch $1500.

There are many Australian-made foods.

Australians love their beer. Various societies have made beers for thousands of years by fermenting a cereal, usually hops. There are many different types of beer, such as stout, ale and lager.

Beers that were brewed by traditional European techniques did not survive well in the hot climate of Australia. But one Bavarian beer lasted well and did not turn sour when it came in contact with the air. This beer was called 'lager-bier', or 'beer for storing'. ('Lager' is the German word for 'store'.) In the 1860s, lager beer became very popular in the United States of America.

By the mid-1880s there had been a few unsuccessful attempts to make lager in Australia. The

Foster brothers arrived in Melbourne from New York in 1886. Mr Sieber, a refrigeration engineer and a brewer with experience in both Germany and America, came with them. His help was invaluable. On 1 February 1889, icy-cold bottles of Foster's Lager were first sold in Melbourne. To promote their beer, the Foster brothers even supplied the hotels with free ice in summer to keep the lager cool. Today Foster's Lager is famous worldwide.

In 1865, a Scot called William Arnott had saved only £14 after years working in the goldfields. So he moved to Newcastle, and opened a bakery. This was a risky move — back then, everybody made their own bread, biscuits and cakes at home. But at that time, Newcastle had a very busy port, with about 800 ships coming in each year to pick up coal. The crews of these ships were ready customers for his bakery. Business was great. He opened William Arnott's Steam Biscuits Factory in 1877. By 1888,

Butter Menthol & Steam Roller

Alfred Allen started making sweets in Fitzroy in Melbourne in 1891, when he was only 20 years old. He was responsible for the Butter Menthol and the Steam Roller. He was so successful that, by 1909, A.W. Allen was the third biggest sweet-making factory in all of Victoria.

Chico Roll

Francis Gerald McEnroe, a caterer from Bendigo, saw another caterer selling Chinese rolls outside the Melbourne Cricket Ground in 1950. He thought he could do better, and tried various ingredients. One version that he sold at the 1951 Wagga Wagga Show had chicken in it, which gave him the name he would call it – Chico Roll. He then tried mutton and various vegetables, until he settled on a mixture of beef, barley, celery, onion, carrot and cabbage.

About 2 million Chico Rolls are sold each month. They look light and crisp, but some people say they don't taste like that. Some unkind people have compared them to deep-fried linoleum with soggy stuff inside!

it was sending 30 tonnes of biscuits each week to Sydney by steamship. To get enough milk for their Milk Arrowroot biscuits, they owned their own dairy farms and some 200 cows. By 1890, Arnott's 300 workers were making 18 different types of biscuits.

Unfortunately, William Arnott never tasted Arnott's most famous and popular biscuit — the SAO. Historians are not too sure what SAO stands for. Some people say it stands for Salvation Army Order — perhaps influenced by William's son, Arthur, who worked with the Salvation Army. Another story is that Leslie, another of William's

13 children, saw a faded sign that originally said 'SAND SOAP'. It had faded to leave only the letters S-A-O visible. Leslie apparently thought that SAO would be a great name for a biscuit.

We will probably never know how the name SAO came about. But we do know that the SAO was first manufactured by his sons in 1906, five years after he died.

The next great food invention was the lamington. Originally, the lamington was just a clever way to recycle slightly dried-out sponge cake that was a day or two old. The cake was iced with an apricot jam or a lemon cheese spread and folded over so that this moist layer was in the middle. It was then cut into little cubes, iced with chocolate, and finally rolled in coconut. Lamingtons first showed up in cookery books in 1914, although they had begun to appear in outback kitchens around 1900.

There are two theories about the name 'lamington'. One theory is that it comes from Baron Lamington, the Governor of Queensland from 1895 to 1901. On his visits to the outback, he would be served some of these new cakes and he must have liked them. The other theory is that the word lamington comes from the word 'lamina' (meaning a thin layer), referring to the moist layer in the middle of the cube.

Vegemite was the great food invention of 1923. Fred Walker wanted to sell a vitamin supplement to the Australian public. He started up by buying excess brewer's yeast from the Carlton & United Brewery. This yeast was being thrown away, even though it is one of the richest sources of the B-group vitamins. Walker asked a 30-year-old chemist, Cyril Percy Callister, to do something with the yeast, this unwanted waste product from the breweries.

Callister spent a year experimenting before he

came up with a vitamin-enriched paste made from yeast, vegetables and salt. He got the goodness out of the yeast cells by splitting them open with enzymes. Walker Foods released Vegemite in 1923 — and it immediately flopped. Nobody bought it!

At the time, there was a competing product on the market called Marmite. In 1928, Vegemite was renamed Parwill (Pa will) to make it seem really different from Marmite (Ma might). But Parwill did no better than Vegemite.

So Walker Foods went back to the Vegemite name. This time, they spent big — they gave away Walker cheese with the jars of Vegemite and gave away cars in Vegemite competitions. Gradually, the sales of Vegemite picked up.

But a free advertising boost came in 1939 with World War II, when the British Medical Association officially proclaimed that Vegemite was an excellent source of the B vitamins. In World War II, Vegemite was included in the Australian Army ration packs. Now the buying public could firmly believe that Vegemite was good for you.

The Walker company even ran advertisements saying: *Vegemite fights for the men up north! If you are one of those who don't need Vegemite medicinally, then thousands of invalids and babies are asking you to deny yourself for the time being.*

One of the most popular Australian radio advertisements ever made was the Vegemite jingle:

Kraft Cheese Trommel

Cheese has been around for thousands of years. You start off with milk and you ferment it. Soon you'll have solids (curd) *and* liquid (whey), which have to be separated. It has always been hard work to drain off the whey and cut the curd up, especially in very large amounts.

But in 1937, Doug Lambert at the Kraft Walker Cheese Company in Melbourne came up with a machine that could do this hard work. This machine, the 'trommel', was patented by Kraft and soon put into use across the world.

We're happy little Vegemites, as bright as bright can be,
We all enjoy our Vegemite, for breakfast, lunch and tea,
We all enjoy our Vegemite, we all adore our Vegemite,
It puts a rose in every cheek.

This jingle was first released in 1954. It was so successful that it was modified for television in 1956, and then re-released in 1988.

When Kraft bought out Fred Walker's business, they also bought his secret recipe. However, after a while they had to change the recipe. In 1981, *Choice* magazine reported that Vegemite was 10% salt by weight! Because of the recent awareness that too much salt in the diet can cause high blood pressure, they had to reduce the amount of salt. The salt level was reduced to about 4%, which is still high enough to stop mould forming. Today, nine out of every 10 Australian homes carry a jar of Vegemite — and yet it is virtually unknown overseas.

In 1934, Nestles introduced Milo Tonic Food into Australia. This product was named after the original Milo, a wrestler who lived about 2400 years ago. In those days a wrestling match went on until one of the wrestlers died! So the young wrestlers took their training programs very seriously. At the age of 12, Milo came across a cow that had just given birth to a calf. He picked up the calf and ran around his training field with the calf on his shoulders. He started doing this every day. Every day, that calf grew a little bit heavier, and every day, he became a little stronger.

By the age of 18, Milo was a giant of a man. Every day he would carry the calf, now a full–grown bull, on his shoulders around the training field. Milo won many prizes for his wrestling — he even won gold medals at the original Olympic Games! In those days, the average person was lucky to live to the age of 30. Because of his build and strength, Milo survived and died peacefully at the age of 70.

The pavlova was created by Bert (Herbert) Sasche in 1934 (some books say 1935). He was the chef at the Esplanade Hotel in Perth. The pavlova was named in honour of the famous Russian dancer Anna Pavlova, who had stayed at the hotel and who had died some four years earlier. Pavlova was very light on her feet, and appeared to 'float' through the air — so the food named after her was supposed to be very light.

Bert Sasche had been approached by the licensee of the hotel, Mrs Elizabeth Paxton. She wanted to make her hotel the only place to be for afternoon teas — and she wanted to attract people with something new, different and very special. Sasche experimented with different ingredients for a month. He said to a reporter: 'I had always regretted that the meringue cake was invariably too hard and crusty, so I set out to create something that could have a crunchy top and would cut like marshmallow.' So he tried adding cornflour and vinegar to the usual ingredients.

A pavlova is a desert mostly made of meringue — hard on the outside and soft on the inside. Bert's original ingredients were 6 ounces of sugar, six egg whites, an ounce of cornflour, a small dessertspoon of vinegar, a few drops of vanilla essence, a reasonable-sized pinch of cream of tartar, one-third of a pint of cream, and three or four passion fruit. The top is usually decorated with whipped cream and fresh fruit of the season, such as strawberries, passion fruit or kiwi fruit. It should taste fantastic — even better than fairy floss — and should melt in your mouth. There should be about a centimetre of crust, which holds the delicious soft interior together. It is hard on the outside because it is baked

Pavlova is NOT Australian!

The New Zealanders claim that *they* invented the pavlova, several years before Bert Sasche came up with his version in 1934. The book *Home Cookery for New Zealand* appeared in 1926. It had a recipe for a 'Meringue with Fruit Filling'. In 1927, the same recipe was renamed the pavlova.

Another New Zealand cookbook, *Aunt Daisy's Cookbook*, was published in 1926. It has a recipe for a three-egg 'Pavlova Cake'.

in a very hot oven for a very short time. If you bake it too long, you end up with a meringue rock!

Sasche presented the cake to the hotel management, and they said, 'It is as light as Pavlova.'

After 200 years, the only native Australian food that is regularly eaten is the macadamia nut. Australia imports frozen fish fingers from the Atlantic countries, yet we are the world's largest producer of abalone and squid. The reason for our lack of national foods has something to do with the way in which our society developed.

When you talk about growing or using food on our planet, there are three types of society you need to look at.

The first type is the hunter–gatherer society, such as the Aborigines had in Australia before the invasion by Europeans. Animals are hunted for food, and fruit and nuts are gathered from bushes.

The second type of society is agricultural. In North America, the American Indians grew more than 2000 different plants, including sweet potato, corn and pumpkin. They even invented what are now classic American dishes, such as roast turkey and clam chowder. In an agricultural society, the people live close to the land, planting their crops and herding their animals. Normally, what they eat is what they grow.

The third type of society is the industrial society. In this type of society, food comes from factories. The factories are supplied by giant farms, which usually grow just one product, such as corn or wheat.

In Australia, we have never had an agricultural society. We are the only country on the planet to have gone straight from a hunter–gatherer society to an industrial society. Perhaps this is why we have had such a mishmash of cuisines.

Violet Crumble Bar

In 1923 Abel Hoadley whipped up the very first Violet Crumble Bar.

At that time, his main line of business was making jams and pickles. However, in each growing season, he would have surpluses of fruit and other supplies. He started making different sweets to use up this excess.

The Violent crumble bar...

But over the last twenty years, there have been enormous changes in what we eat. We now have fewer biscuits and more low-fat milk, processed fresh chicken, specialty breads with a high fibre content and ready-cut, vacuum-packed vegetables.

We have moved away from the old 'standard' meal of a large amount of red meat and three vegetables. Already, 64% of Australians eat a stir-fried meal twice a week. Stir-frying is healthier because it uses a greater variety of vegetables. The vegetables are cooked for a very short time, conserving more of the vitamins in the food. More people are eating rice and pasta, instead of only potato.

We now have a variety of distinctive, and uniquely Australian, foods.

Mawson and Marriage

Sir Douglas Mawson, that man whose face we used to see wearing a balaclava on the $100 note, was the first man ever to propose marriage by radio. He also accidentally discovered the windiest place on our planet!

He was born in Bradford, England, in 1882, and came to Australia with his parents when he was just two years old. He graduated in mining engineering from the University of Sydney in 1902, then became a lecturer in geology at the University of Adelaide in 1905.

He went to Antarctica for the first time in 1907 with Sir Ernest Shackleton's expedition. It was then that he took part in the first successful climb of the active volcano Mount Erebus. He was also on the expedition that first found the Magnetic South Pole — on 16 January 1909.

He was later invited by Captain R.F. Scott of Britain to join Scott's expedition of 1910 to 1912, which would attempt to reach the geographic South Pole (which is a long way from the Magnetic South Pole — see box, Earth's Wandering Magnetic Poles), but Mawson refused — he wanted to lead the first Australasian team to Antarctica.

In winter, Antarctica actually 'grows' as the ice packs build up around it. After the end of winter, the ice packs slowly begin to break apart. If you're on a ship you have to wait for the early treacherous ice to get out of the way before you can sail to a safe landing on the shore. Waiting for the ice floes to clear during spring can rob you of precious time that you want to use for exploration. So, Mawson decided that the expedition would land in late summer, spend a winter in Antarctica and then, as soon the weather cleared, they would start exploring.

Under his leadership, the 1911 to 1914 Australasian Antarctic Expedition left on 2 December 1911. He had a few experienced explorers and some 25 young graduates from Australian and New Zealand universities with him. They sailed along the coast of Antarctica looking for some bare rock on which to build their winter home. After thousands of kilometres of sailing, they finally found some bare rock in a bay which Mawson named Commonwealth Bay. They didn't wonder why this particular patch of rock was bare of ice and snow — they were just glad that it was bare. They needed bare rock to build on.

The expedition went ashore with all the supplies and began to build a small wooden shack. They knew that the Antarctic winds could be extremely strong, so they built their home for the winter very tightly indeed. They built it in the same way in which a carpenter builds a fine piece of furniture —

This Story May Not be Totally True!!

The story I have written about Mawson differs slightly from stories you will read in the history books. However, it's worth telling, because it was told to me by one of the men who was on that first expedition in 1911 — Mr Webb. (Mr Webb was with the group who looked for the Magnetic South Pole.) He told his story to me and some 400 other people on a Dick Smith jumbo 747 flight down to the Antarctic and back again.

with many interlocking tongue-and-groove joints in the wood. Then they nailed the whole thing together, to make it extra tight. Finally, they drilled holes 1 metre deep into the rock and then they bolted their house onto the rock. Now they had a house that was as strong as a house could be *and* was securely bolted to solid rock.

Their ship sailed away. They were left alone for the winter, which set in with a vengeance. Their toilet was only 5 metres away from the front door of their hut, but the howling blizzard that raged continuously throughout the freezing winter night was so severe that they literally could not see a hand in front of their faces. They had to follow ropes that led to the toilet and back. Their hut was covered with metres of snow. But in spite of this snow on the roof, a perpetual flurry of fine snow crystals whistled through the air of their hut. Inside the hut it was cold, wet and windy.

While they were building their house they had also built some machines that could measure wind velocity up to 300 kph. These machines were often torn apart by the blasting wind and would have to be repaired each time. Gradually, Mawson and his team realised the terrible truth. They had built their hut on the windiest spot on the entire planet earth! They now knew the reason why the rock was bare — the wind blew away the snow and ice!

Of course, it wasn't that windy all the time. But, according to their wind-measuring machines, during winter the wind velocity averaged 65 kph for 40% of the time!

The conditions were terrible. Mawson wrote in his diary for 19 July 1912: *Blizzard, very hard. About one of the worst we have had. Dogs are often found frozen to the ground, especially in the store. They whine piteously, for they can't move.*

Finally, the terrible winter finished and the sun climbed over the horizon. Now it was time to work. Mawson's expedition divided itself into several separate teams and started preparing for different journeys.

Windy Antarctic

Antarctica is the windiest continent on Earth. Its ice has the shape of a giant, flattened ice-cream cone — about 4000 km across, and a few kilometres high. Air from the upper atmosphere falls to the ground around the middle of Antarctica. Then it flows outwards in all directions towards the coast down a 2000-km-long hill. (The same thing happens at home. When you open the fridge door, you can feel cool air rolling out of the fridge onto your feet — if you put a lit candle on the floor, the flame will flicker.)

So, for most of the time in the Antarctic, there's a continuous 30 kph wind rolling down from the Pole.

On 9 December 1960, wind gusts of between 225 and 250 kph destroyed a Beaver aircraft at Mawson Station.

The wind can destroy, but you can use wind to make electricity. Because there is so much wind in Antarctica, the wind turbines will run almost continuously. The cost of electricity from the wind is about six times cheaper than electricity from diesel generators.

The Americans have had four 3-kilowatt turbines running since 1985. One of their wind turbines has survived temperatures down to -60°C and wind speeds up to 300 kph. One Australian 12-kilowatt wind turbine is designed to produce its full power with winds of between 45 and 80 kph, but has survived winds of 324 kph!

One team went inland to search for the Magnetic South Pole to see how far it had moved. (They knew it moved because of compasses. Scientists compare compass readings from year to year.) At that time it still lay under the ice, not under the water offshore as it does now. (See box, Earth's Wandering Magnetic Poles.) A second team set off along the coast to travel in a big circle, exploring the inland, before returning to the base.

A third team was made up of the Australian Mawson, the 22-year-old British lieutenant Belgrave Ninnis, of the Royal Inniskilling Fusiliers, and the

High Antarctica

Antarctica is the highest continent on Earth – about 2300 metres above sea level. This is because of the ice. In fact, 98% of Antarctica is covered with ice.

The average thickness of the ice is about 2000 metres. The ice is so heavy that it has pushed down the land underneath by about 560 metres. (You might think that land is solid, but it is actually 'plastic', and will move slowly under pressure.) If all the ice were removed, the land would slowly rise again. Most of East Antarctica would be above sea level, while most of West Antarctica would be a shallow sea.

The highest point in Antarctica is Vinson Massif – it is 5140 metres above sea level.

28-year-old Dr Xavier Mertz, a Swiss skiing champion and a law graduate. They set off on 10 November 1912 to explore the area east of their base. They had 17 dogs pulling their three sleds. Each sled was about 3.5 metres long and their total load was over 770 kg. They abandoned one sled after they had used up all its supplies.

Their progress was good, considering the conditions. On a good day they could travel 30 km. If the weather was bad, they couldn't travel and had to stay in their tent.

On 14 December, after they had travelled 500 km, Ninnis fell down a crevasse to his death. Their main sled, with most of the food and supplies and most of their strongest dogs, was lost with him.

Suddenly things looked very grim. There was no food for the remaining dogs, which were barely strong enough to pull the sled.

Cold Antarctica

Antarctica is the coldest continent on Earth. The coldest temperature ever recorded outdoors (not in a laboratory) was measured at Vostok Station at a height of 3505 metres on 21 July 1983. It was -89.2°C!

Even in the warmest month, the average temperature there is -33°C. In fact, the warmest temperature ever measured at Vostok Station is -21°C.

However, on the coast, it's much warmer, with average temperatures ranging between -15 and -10°C.

Mawson and Mertz had to turn back. For food, they had to eat the dogs. They started with the weakest dog, George. They fried him for breakfast and then started home. The next day, they fed what was left of George to the remaining five dogs. The next dog they ate was Mary. As they went on, the dogs had so little muscle on them that they had to eat the livers — the only meaty parts left. Mawson wrote: *It was a happy relief when the liver appeared ...*

Luckily, Mawson was a very strong man with a very rugged constitution. He and Mertz started pulling the sled home themselves. By Christmas Day 1912, they were down to their last dog — and they

Dry Antarctica

Antarctica is the driest continent on Earth — in fact, it's one of the world's great deserts. The water from clouds doesn't fall as liquid because it's so cold there — it falls as snow. The weather scientists melt the snow and measure how much water it generates.

Inland, the average amount of water falling from the sky (precipitation) is only 50 mm per year. The coast is wetter, with an annual precipitation of 380 mm.

Ironically, 90% of all the fresh water on the planet is locked up in Antarctica as ice — about 30 million cubic kilometres! If all this ice melted, the sea level would rise by about 60 metres.

Daytime and Night-time

Most of the world has 365 days in each year, and the Sun rises and sets on each of those days. Antarctica (and the Arctic) are different. At the South Pole, in the middle of summer, the Sun is continually above the horizon for five months. In the middle of winter, the Sun is continually below the horizon for five months. In spring and autumn, there is a twilight that lasts for about one month.

were still 250 km away from the base. They had a feast of biscuits and dog's brain: *Had a great breakfast of Ginger's brains and thyroids.*

Then things got worse.

Liver is a rich food; it has lots of vitamin A. But you can have too much of a good thing. Mawson and Mertz didn't know it, but the vitamin A was slowly poisoning them both. Mertz was more susceptible to the huge amounts of vitamin A they were both eating and began to get very sick. Mertz began to suffer from peeling skin, frostbite, vomiting, diarrhoea and convulsive fits.

On the night of 6 January his fits were so bad that as he thrashed around in the tent, he broke the central tent pole! Mawson was very depressed, and wrote: *A long and wearisome night. If only I could go on ... But I have to stop with Xavier and he does not appear to be improving. I cannot leave him ... It is very hard for me — to be within 160 kilometres of the hut ... both our chances are going now ...*

Mertz died the next night. Mawson buried him, using two sled runners as a cross to mark his grave. Mawson was in a bad way himself. His diary says: *My whole body is rotting ... frost-bitten fingertips, festerings ... skin coming off whole body ...* By January 24 he was writing: *Both my hands have shed the skin in large sheets.* His feet were in a bad way, too. He later wrote: *The sight was shocking, for the thick skin of the soles had separated as a complete layer, and abundant watery fluid had escaped into the bandages. And ahead lay the broken surface of the glacier.*

There was another problem — navigation. He realised that his compass was strongly affected by being so close to the Magnetic South Pole and that it was not always giving correct readings, and his watch kept stopping. But his skill was so good that he was within 300 metres of his planned path.

He had been gone a long time and the other members of his expedition were worried about him. They put up a pile of stones on the hill overlooking the base station. Just underneath the stones was a hole carved into the ice containing food and a place to sleep.

By incredible good luck and good navigation, Mawson came across the pile of stones. Even though he could see the base station in the distance, he had

Earth's Disappearing Magnetic Poles

Two very strange things are happening to the Earth's magnetic field. It is getting weaker, and a new pair of Magnetic North and South Poles is growing!

The Earth's magnetic field has weakened by 10% over the last 140 years. If it keeps on falling at this rate, there will be no magnetic field at all in a few thousand years. The magnetic field protects us from the radiation of deep space, and is used by crabs, pigeons and whales for navigation.

A second Magnetic North Pole is growing in Siberia, while a second Magnetic South Pole is gradually building up strength in the ocean off the coast of Brazil.

What the scientists think happens in a magnetic field reversal is that the magnetic field of the Earth gradually falls to zero and the Magnetic North and South Poles swap over. Then the magnetic field builds up again. The last reversal of the magnetic field happened about 700,000 years ago. Maybe this new pair of Magnetic Poles is part of the chaos that happens as the Earth's magnetic field falls to zero.

If it does happen that the magnetic field falls completely to zero, then all the compasses will be pointless!

to strengthen himself with real food to be able to go on. He ate and slept in what the other expedition members called 'Aladdin's Cave'.

He woke the next morning invigorated. He climbed out of his cave and, to his horror, saw his supply ship steaming away from the base. In a panic, he rushed down the hill back to the base. As he got closer, he could see a radio antenna above the

Earth's Wandering Magnetic Poles

The Magnetic South Pole actually wanders a few kilometres each year (unlike the Geographic South Pole, which is relatively fixed, although it does move a little bit). It moves about 8 km in a northwest direction each year. In 1996, the Magnetic South Pole was located off the coast of Antarctica, near Adélie Land. It has shifted about 880 km since Mawson first discovered it. I flew over the South Magnetic Pole in a jumbo 747 that Dick Smith had chartered (the same flight on which Mr Webb told us the story of Mawson). The needles on the magnetic compasses in the 747 all pointed straight down into the ground when we were right over the Magnetic South Pole.

In 1993, the Magnetic North Pole was west of Ellef Ringnes Island, in the extreme northern part of Canada. The Magnetic North Pole has been very closely watched by Canadian scientists for the last 35 years. Each year, it travels north some 24 km, and west some 5.7 km.

hut — the ship had bought a radio down to Antarctica. Inside the hut there was only a skeleton crew left. The radio operator called up the ship to get it to come back and get him. The ship did turn around, but the headwinds were too great; even though the ship steamed at full speed towards the shore, the wind gradually blew it back out to sea. With a heavy heart he settled down to spend another winter in the Antarctic.

By the time he got back to the base station, on 8 February 1913, he had eaten enough vitamin A to kill the average person five times over. Only his rugged constitution, and sheer willpower, kept him going.

Mawson didn't look good after his terrible journey. The vitamin A poisoning and the starvation had taken a toll. He weighed only 48 kg (about half his normal weight); he had yellow skin and he was almost bald. It was while he was in this condition that he 'spoke' to his wife-to-be, Francisca Adriana (Paquita) Delprat, via the radio operator, who used Morse code. Voice communication did not exist at that time. It was then that he made the first-ever proposal of marriage on the two-way radio.

Francisca accepted his proposal.

During the following winter the radio operator went mad. He sent Morse code messages back to Australia, saying that his companions had gone crazy and were trying to lock him up. Once his

Discovery of Antarctica

The ancient Greeks thought that there had to be a giant continent in the Southern Hemisphere to balance the land masses in the Northern Hemisphere.

Captain Cook sailed right around Antarctica in his expedition of 1772 to 1775. Probably the first people actually to see Antarctica were the American sealer Nathaniel Palmer and the British naval officers Edward Bransfield and William Smith. They separately saw the tip of the Antarctic Peninsula in 1820.

The first person to land in Antarctica was another American sealer, Captain John Davis, who landed on 7 February 1821. (However, another encyclopaedia claims that Leonard Kristensen and C.E. Borchgrevink of Norway were the first to land in Antarctica, in 1894 or 1895.) On 14 December 1911, the Norwegian Roald Amundsen and his team of four were the first to reach the geographic South Pole.

companions discovered that *he* had gone crazy, of course they *had to* lock him up!

When Mawson returned to Australia, he married Francisca, who was the daughter of Guillaume Delprat, the General Manager of Broken Hill Proprietary Limited (BHP). (Read about Delprat and BHP in the story 'Floating Metals' in *Ears, Gears & Gadgets.*)

Mawson went to England in 1914 and was honoured by being made a knight. His expedition had achieved its goals — they had mapped over 1500 km of the Antarctic coast and had travelled some 500 km inland.

In 1920, he was made Professor of Geology at the University of Adelaide. From 1929 to 1931, he led the combined British, Australian and New Zealand Antarctic Research Expedition.

On 13 February 1954, the first permanent Australian research station was set up in Antarctica. It was named Mawson Station in his honour. When he died in 1958, he was given an official state funeral.

Surf Lifesaving

The first person to be saved by an official Australian surf lifesaving reel was also the first person to fly a plane across the Pacific Ocean.

But many years after the lifesaving incident, the ocean still took his life.

Charlie Smith, of Yates Street, North Sydney, was only 10 years old when he and his cousin, Rupert Swallow, were hauled out of a wild Bondi surf early in 1907. Lifesavers used the newly invented reel to pull them back to safety. The kids thanked their saviours with a 'We're all right, thanks' and a 'Sorry to cause all the trouble', before they ran away.

They were very lucky. The lifesaving reel had just been introduced on 23 December 1906, in a public demonstration at Bondi Beach. That was only 11 days before their accident!

Charlie Smith was very interested in airplanes, and became Sir Charles Kingsford Smith ('Smithy' to his mates) — Australia's most famous aviator. He set many flight records. They included the first America–Australia flight; the first crossing of the Atlantic Ocean from east to west; the first non-stop crossing of Australia; and the first round-the-world flight with an equatorial crossing.

But in November 1935, Sir Charles and his plane, the *Lady Southern Cross*, disappeared off the coast of Burma. The only clue to his disappearance ever found was washed up on a beach — a wheel from his plane.

In Western society, swimming was not really popular before the 1700s. The first written instructions on how to revive a drowned person appeared in 1755. It took until 1816 before the first description of how to save people appeared. In 1891, the Royal Life Saving Service started operations in Britain. In 1914, the American Red Cross publicised methods of resuscitation across America.

There are three basic ways to rescue a drowning person — throw a rope or something that floats to them, row out to them in a boat, or swim out to them. Swimming out to a drowning person is the most dangerous to the rescuer — because of the risk that the drowning person will panic and pull the rescuer under.

Australia has the ideal climate for people to spend time outdoors. Depending on your location and the water temperature, you can comfortably swim for some seven months of the year. Most Australian children can swim by the age of eight.

Surfing got off to a late start in Australia, because there were laws forbidding people to bathe in the daylight hours between six a.m. and eight p.m. One alderman from a seaside suburb hated seeing people swimming, and said, 'the rapture of the lonely shore, the quiet most essential to residential happiness, is sadly interfered with by these surf bathers. I can no longer take my daughters for a walk by the waves

Surfing History

Surfing started in Hawaii – the nobility of that country surfed on long wooden boards. In 1788, Captain Cook wrote that the Hawaiians had surfing competitions. But the European missionaries thought that surfing was so much fun that it was immoral! By 1821, the missionaries had almost completely stopped the Hawaiians from surfing.

But by 1920 surfing had started again and the Hawaiian Olympic swimming champion Duke Kahanamoku started up the first surfing club in Waikiki. Before that, in 1915, he had visited Australia and had introduced surfing here. Today there are some 300,000 surfers in Australia.

because the recumbent nakedness is too indecent, the return to nature too pronounced altogether.'

And this was when the law forced people to be covered from their necks to their elbows and knees! But many people thought this was a stupid law, and deliberately broke it publicly. They dared the police to come and arrest them when they bathed in the evening after eight p.m. or earlier than six a.m. As it happened, a religious man, the rector of St Mary's Church in Waverley, Sydney, was finally prosecuted for breaking this law.

There had to be a way for keen surfers to legally surf whenever they wanted. A group of friends formed a surf lifesaving club and trained themselves in rescue procedures. In February 1906, the Bondi Surf Bathers' Life Saving Club sprang into existence. The surfers thought it would be hard for the authorities to argue against a club that was there to save lives! Membership card number one was in the name of Lyster Ormsby, who was one of the main organisers of the club.

Soon, other groups of surfers around Sydney formed themselves into similar life saving clubs.

Surfing Waves

According to the 1993 *Guinness Book of Records*, the longest ridable surf waves are in Mexico. About five times each year, the conditions in Matanchen Bay near San Blas, Nayarit, are such that surfers can ride a wave for about 1.7 km!

The highest consistently ridable waves are in Waimea Bay, Hawaii – up to 10 metres high.

Shark Started Tyre Business

Sharks have always had very bad publicity, but they are not that dangerous. Each year, over the whole planet, only 50 people are taken by sharks. But 150 people are killed by lightning each year. So if you're down at the beach, and you can see shark fins in the water and then a wild electrical storm comes along the sand towards you, you'd probably be safer in the water!

Frank Beaurepaire is one person who *benefited* from a shark attack. His now-massive car tyre business started with a shark attack! In 1922, Frank was at the peak of his swimming career. He had represented Australia on six overseas trips, had set 14 world swimming records and had won over 200 titles. In November of that year, he bravely dived into the water to try to rescue Milton Coughlan while Milton was actually being attacked by a shark at Coogee Beach in Sydney. Tragically Milton died on the way to the hospital. Even so, the people of New South Wales were so impressed by his bravery that the government gave Frank a reward of £1000. He used this to set up a car tyre business, which evolved into Beaurepaires Tyres.

On 18 October 1907, these clubs formed themselves into the New South Wales Surf Bathers Association.

Before surf lifesavers and their safety equipment were available on the beach, swimmers were always getting into difficulty. At Sydney's Manly Beach alone, records tell us 17 people drowned before 1902. People who had never seen the sea before would arrive at the beach and dive straight in! The tides and rips would take them completely by surprise and wash them right out to sea.

Some beaches had a wooden pole in the centre of the beach, close to the water. Right next to the pole was a rope attached to a circular life buoy. It didn't work very well, because you simply couldn't throw the life buoy far enough out into the surf to reach the drowning person. If you tried to wear the life buoy while you plunged into the surf to rescue somebody, you soon found out that the life buoy was almost impossible to swim in. The pole–rope–life buoy system was hopeless.

Lyster Ormsby and his offsider, Warrant Officer John Bond, experimented with different ways of rescuing people who were in distress in the waves. The first thing they did was to swap the cork life buoy for a ship's life jacket. The life jacket was bulky, but at least it was possible to swim while wearing it. Once you reached the drowning swimmer, your fellow surfers back on land would pull you back with the rope.

Ormsby and Bond chose strong swimmers and trained them in rescue techniques. They also tried out different ropes, to see which ones were the safest to use in different types of surf.

And then *somebody* (we don't know who) came up with the surf lifesaving reel.

Ormsby and Bond claimed that *they* personally designed, and made a model of, the first ever lifesaving reel. They also claimed that they then showed their original model to a coachmaker named G.H. Olding to get him to build a full-size version. Ormsby and Bond claimed that they knew what they wanted, but they didn't have the necessary technical skills to make it.

Olding, who was also a regular surf swimmer, told a very different story. He always claimed that the entire idea and design were his alone! He wrote that

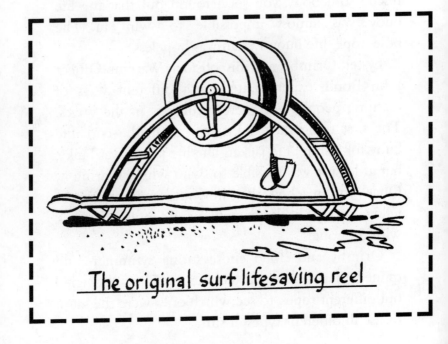

The original surf lifesaving reel

The Lady Southern Cross

Even something as simple as taking off was dangerous when Kingsford-Smith was on a mission to break another record. The plane's specifications were that it could carry a pilot and navigator, 10 passengers and enough fuel to cover 600 km. A maximum weight of 4.7 tonnes was allowed for. But on occasions, it weighed 7.2 tonnes (2.5 tonnes too much) when it took off, thanks to all the extra fuel.

he took *strong exception to the statement that Mr Bond, or anybody else, was the inventor of the lifesaving reel ... no plan, design, measurement or any idea was submitted to me ... I did not start until I had evolved in my mind a satisfactory plan.*

We'll probably never really know who designed the lifesaving reel. But all accounts agree on one fact — it was Olding who actually *made* the first lifesaving reel. He used a cedar drum mounted on a wooden frame. A handle attached to the side of the cedar drum was used to pay out a rope line, or reel it back onto the drum. The rope line was attached to a belt, worn by the best swimmer in the club. He would race across the sand, dive into the water, and then swim out to the drowning person. The rest of the lifesaving team fed the line out, until the lifesaver reached the person in

Black Sunday at Bondi Beach

At Bondi Beach, Black Sunday is always remembered as being Sunday, 6 February 1938. It was a hot day on a weekend, and thousands of people had come to Bondi Beach to jump in the water and get away from the heat.

Suddenly, three enormous waves pounded the beach, followed by another three huge, freak waves. Within seconds, more than 200 people who had been on a sandbank were carried hundreds of metres out to sea by the rip.

By an amazing coincidence, 70 members of the Bondi Beach Surf Bathers' Life Saving Club were on the beach. They were training for some races. They immediately raced into the raging torrent and began to rescue people. Time after time, they plunged into the water.

Hundreds of lives were saved, but five people died on that terrible day.

---

trouble. Then the team would haul them both back to the shore.

Australia has an excellent surf lifesaving record. Since the introduction of the surf lifesaving reel in 1907, over 380,000 rescues have been made at Bondi Beach alone. Our safety reputation is known all over the world. In fact, Wollongong, 80 km south of Sydney, was the first place in the world to have a shark plane. We even have groups of Japanese lifesavers coming to train and learn from our lifesaving clubs.

People are always getting into difficulties in the surf. On just one day, Christmas Day 1996, surf lifesavers rescued 305 people at one beach — North Cronulla Beach. On 23 March 1997, more than 65 people were rescued at Bondi Beach. According to a senior Bondi lifeguard, Mr Lawrie Williams, about 125 people had been rescued each week for the prior three months.

By 1995, there were 260 surf lifesaving clubs in Australia, with a total membership of more than 73,000. Thanks to the surf lifesaving reel, the annual report of almost every surf lifesaving club in Australia finishes with the words *No lives lost while patrols on duty*.

Aboriginal Vision

Some Aboriginal tribes have the sharpest vision of any humans ever measured on our planet. But what is really remarkable is that they keep this super-sharp vision right into their old age. One of their other skills is that they remember patterns much better than non-Aboriginal people can.

Vision is measured by two numbers. Average vision is measured as 6/6. That means that you can see clearly at a distance of 6 metres what the average person can see clearly at 6 metres. (Twenty/twenty is just the American version of this — they measure their distances in feet, not metres.)

The first number, or the number on top, is the distance at which you can read a standard chart, measured in metres. The number on the bottom is the distance at which the average person can read the same chart.

Vision of 3/6 is below average; 3/6 means that even though the *average person* can see an object sharply at 6 metres, *you* have to be 3 metres away to see that same object clearly; 3/6 means that you have to wear glasses. Some people are lucky — they have vision that is better than average. If your vision is 6/5, you can see objects at 6 metres that the average person can only see clearly at 5 metres.

Some groups of people, such as the Aborigines, and racing car drivers, have much sharper vision than other groups!

There is a tribe of Aborigines in Western Australia whose average vision is 6/1.5! This means that they can see at 6 metres what the average person can see at only 1.5 metres. If a non-Aboriginal Australian could see a tree a few hundred

Brain Outside the Skull

The retina of the eye is actually a part of your brain that has pushed its way out through little holes in the skull.

Light Equals Life

Without light, there would be no life on our planet. Green plants turn light into electricity. This is called photosynthesis. This electricity is used as a power supply by the plant to turn carbon dioxide into carbohydrates. The plant then uses these carbohydrates to make itself bigger. (We humans eat three types of food – carbohydrate, protein and fat.)

Plants are at the bottom of virtually every food chain on our planet. So without plants, we would have no life.

metres away, a sharp-eyed Aborigine could see a small animal on the ground in the shade of that tree!

You can see that it's handy for young, healthy and strong nomadic tribal people to have sharp vision. Not only can they see an animal that is far away, but they are also strong enough to chase the animal and kill it for food.

But, as a Western Australian study shows, it's not just the young people who have this sharp vision, it's the tribal elders as well. Why should the Aboriginal elders have sharp vision, when in practically every other group of people the older people have poorer vision? How could they evolve so that the whole tribe have sharp vision, even into old age?

Maybe this Western Australian tribe got their sharp vision because they were a very nomadic people. (Other Aborigines who lived in fertile and lush surroundings would have been less nomadic. All the food they wanted would have been close at hand.)

The ancestors of these Aborigines in Western Australia would have spent much of their time travelling across deserts. Western Australia is big — about 2,525,500 square kilometres. It has half a dozen different deserts. Desert just means a biggish place without running water. Some of the deserts have bare sand dunes, while others have dry lakes, small shrubs, long grasses, trees, and so on.

The Third Eye

We all know that most animals on the planet have two eyes. But some reptiles and amphibians have a third eye, along the centre line of the body, usually on the top of their head.

This third eye is often fairly primitive, but lizards have a fairly sophisticated third eye. The lizard cornea on the third eye is not transparent like ours, or like their other two eyes, but is translucent – this means that it passes light, but not a clear image. The lizard's third eye detects the length of the day as it changes through the seasons – short in winter and long in summer. The lizard uses this information to organise aspects of its life, such as knowing when to have babies.

Near-sightedness and Far-sightedness

If you are *near-sighted*, you can see things clearly that are close to you, but distant objects are a blur. Inside your eyeball, the image of a close object lands *on* the retina, so it's sharp. But the image of a distant object lands *in front of* the retina. The beams of light then spread out from this point *in front of* the retina to make a circle *on* the retina. So you have a fuzzy image on the retina.

When you are *far-sighted*, the difference is that the image of close objects lands *behind* the retina. Far objects are in focus.

One type of desert looks different from another type of desert. But once you're inside one desert, one bit of that desert looks very similar to any other bit of that same desert.

We're not too sure why these Aborigines have kept their sharp vision into old age, but here's one theory.

You would need very sharp vision to see tiny little bumps on the horizon that were only slightly different from yesterday's tiny little bumps on the horizon. Now, suppose that the tribe would circle through this bit of desert only once every 10 or 20 years. How would they recognise that those tiny bumps meant that a waterhole was nearby? They would need older Aborigines who had been there 10 or 20 years ago, who had a good memory, and who had sharp vision.

Night Vision

The iris is the coloured part at the front of your eye. It opens when it is dark to let more light in, and closes down in bright sunlight to reduce the amount of light. It can vary from 2 to 8 mm in diameter, which means it can adjust the amount of light falling into the eyeball by about 16 times.

But changing the amount of incoming light is only part of the adjustment your eye makes for seeing in the dark. If you give your eye about 40 minutes to adjust, the retina can become a few thousand times more sensitive to light as well.

You can do an easy experiment with your eyes to show this change in sensitivity. Lie in the dark with your eyes open for at least five minutes. At first the room will seem dark, but then, as your eyes adjust, you'll be able to see more. Then, put one hand over one eye and go out into a well-lit room. Still keeping your hand over one eye, stay in that room for about a minute or so. Then, still keeping that same eye covered, go back into the dark room. Once you're back in the darkness, uncover your other eye.

You'll now find that the eye that was exposed to the light is virtually blind in the darkness, but the eye that has been kept covered can see quite well! Each eye will have a different sensitivity to light.

The Eye

In humans, the eye is a ball about the size of a golf ball — about 25 mm in diameter. The job of the eye is to focus the incoming light rays to make an image on the retina. The retina compresses the information several hundred times and sends it to a part of your brain at the back of your skull.

The light is bent at two places on its path towards the retina. Most of the bending takes place at the front of the eye, at the cornea. The rest of the bending takes place at the lens, which is inside the eye.

When you're young, you can adjust the shape of your lens so you can focus clearly on things that are very close and things that are far away. But as you get older, the lens gradually gets stiffer and can't change shape, so your range of focus is less. The average 10-year-old child can focus clearly on something as close as 7 cm from the front of the eye. By the age of 40 this distance is 16 cm and by the age of 60 it is about 100 cm. The average distance from the eyeball where people hold a book for reading is around 40 cm, so your average 60-year-old needs glasses to be able to read.

The lens of a mouse is so huge that it practically fills the entire eyeball and almost touches the retina. This is because the mouse is very active at night, and wants to be able to gather in as much light as possible.

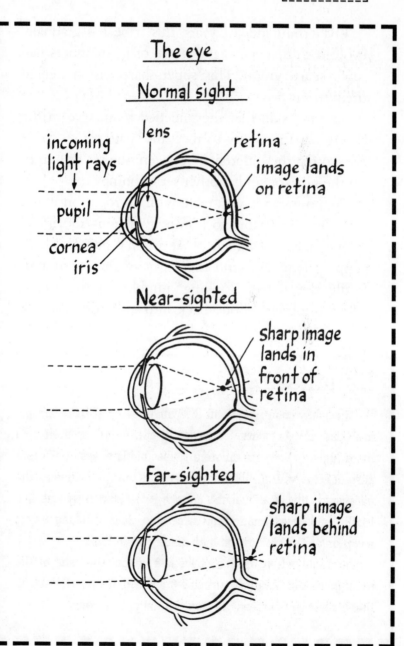

The eye

Normal sight

incoming light rays

lens

retina

image lands on retina

pupil

cornea

iris

Near-sighted

Sharp image lands in front of retina

Far-sighted

sharp image lands behind retina

Over thousands of years, this tribe has gradually evolved so that more and more of its members had super-sharp vision. This super-sharp vision helped them to survive.

Another skill that they needed to survive in the desert was the ability to recognise patterns — to be able to tell the difference between one set of bumps on the horizon and another set of bumps.

Suppose you have a table with 20 rocks on it and you show this table to a bunch of non-Aboriginal people and to a bunch of Aboriginal people. Then, suppose that you send them out of the room and, while they're not looking, jumble up the rocks. Next, bring everybody back into the room, and ask

Blindness

In wealthy countries, about 200 out of every 100,000 people are blind. But in poorer countries, it can be 10 or even 100 times higher. There are different causes of blindness in different parts of the world. Blindness depends on the climate, the geography, the wealth of the country, what sort of germs live locally, and, most importantly, access to clean drinking water, a working toilet system and high quality medical care.

Cataracts, when the lens becomes opaque, are one of the main causes of blindness around the world. It's heartbreaking that a cataract is so easy to cure with simple surgery.

Blinking

You blink every two to ten seconds while you're awake. When you blink, you spread a tiny amount of liquid across the front of your cornea, to keep it wet. It turns out that there is actually a 'blinking centre' in your brain, which tells you how often to blink. But of course, if you're suddenly exposed to sand on a sunny day, or bright sunlight, you'll blink more rapidly. Each day, you will dribble about 1 gram of tears onto the front of your eyeball.

them how many rocks they can put back in their original position and orientation. Non-Aboriginal Australians can do about five rocks correctly, but Aborigines can put back between 15 and 20.

This super-vision of the Aborigines was tested by Professors Fred Hollows and Hugh Taylor. Professor Hollows also discovered a very sad fact. About 5% of Aborigines in the outback will be blind when they die. This blindness is due to an easily preventable disease called trachoma. Hardly any non-Australian Aboriginal people in Australia suffer from this disease, because they have access to running water and a sewage or septic system. But about 50% of Aborigines who don't live in cities have trachoma.

Trachoma was called 'sandy blight' by the early settlers. It's a bacterial disease that firsts attacks the conjunctiva of the eye. The conjunctiva is the thin layer that lines the inside of the eyelids and the white area of the eyeball.

Trachoma is caused by a bacterium called *Chlamydia trachomatis*. The *Chlamydia* invades the conjunctiva. The conjunctiva first becomes swollen and then scarred. If the disease is not treated, the inside of the eyelid will get rough scars growing on it. Each time you blink, these scars rub against the delicate cornea and scratch it! Soon, the clear cornea becomes scarred and opaque, and then you are blind. Seven hundred million people in the world suffer from trachoma — that's about 15% of the entire population of the world. Twenty million people are blind because of trachoma.

This bacteria is quite easy to kill with antibiotics. The hard part is getting the antibiotics to the Aborigines and providing essential health facilities such as clean running water and clean shelter.

Fred Hollows once told me that you cannot have a healthy animal unless you give it enough water. He said that when you raise pigs in quite crowded conditions (like a pig farm), you have to give them 100 litres of water per pig per day. If the pigs don't get access to enough water, they will get dirty, and then sick. He also told me that we humans are quite similar to pigs, from a medical point of view. A heart valve can be taken from a pig and put into a human heart, and work well for decades.

Glasses

Glasses have been around for at least 700 years.

Back in 1268, Roger Bacon wrote about how glass lenses helped vision. At that time, magnifying lenses had already been used for some time in both Europe and China. Tommaso da Modena painted a portrait of Hugh of Provence in 1353. This portrait is famous, because it is the first known painting to show a human being wearing glasses.

Saint Jerome is the Patron Saint of the Guild of Spectacle Makers. This is because in the year 1480, Domenico Ghirlandaio produced a painting in which Saint Jerome was sitting at a desk. A pair of eyeglasses dangled from this desk.

Bifocals, which have a lens on top for distant vision and a lens below for near vision, were invented in 1784 by Benjamin Franklin. If you are older, and your lens has lost much of its youthful flexibility, you can't naturally adjust your vision to see both close and distant objects sharply. It's a bit messy always to have to carry two sets of glasses. So bifocals let you look *up* (using the top of the curved glass) to clearly see distant objects, and *down* (using the bottom) to see close objects.

Pigs and humans have very similar foods in their diet, and, as a result, they have a similar gut.

If the water supply and sewage treatment break down in a city, people quickly get diseases. This is why every family needs a few working taps and access to a working sewage or septic system.

Racing Car Drivers' Vision

You don't normally think of a racing car driver as an athlete. However, physicians at the Indianapolis Methodist Hospital examined some racing car drivers. They found that their reactions were twice as fast as the average person's. They also found that their hearts are as fit as your average Olympic marathon runner. Not only can they accelerate their hearts up to 195 beats per minute for a few minutes, they can even keep them at 175 beats per minute for up to three hours! This ability is very rare.

And they found that many of the drivers have the super-sharp vision that many Aborigines have – 6/1.5.

Fred believed that trachoma in Aborigines would vanish once they had water, working toilet systems and access to medical care.

How ironic that those humans who have the sharpest vision on the planet are also most likely to be blind when they die.

Australian Medicine

Whenever a group of people get together and form a community, one of the first things they do is to find out what medicines there are around them. They look at what the birds and animals eat, and soon they work out what plants can be used as foods, drugs and poisons. Being a healer, in charge of stopping disease and curing the sick, is one of the oldest human professions.

There are two main healing arts — surgery (where you mostly use a knife), and medicine (where you mostly don't use a knife). Our ancestors were skilled in both medicine and surgery.

The Aborigines have been in Australia for over 65,000 years. For much of that time, they had their own healers. The stories that have been passed on from generation to generation are quite clear about how important doctors were in their various tribes.

The Yolngu Tribe of Arnhem Land, like many other peoples around the world, get most of their medicines from plants. But quite a few of their medicines do not come from plants.

For example, they use a special type of white clay to treat an upset stomach. They use red earth to treat chapped lips, and sores and wounds in and around the mouth. They get a special pain-killing drug from the bush cockroach.

They get quite a few medicines from ants. To treat colds and diseases of the chest, they will apply crushed green ants. To treat sore eyes, they will set fire to a particular ant's nest to be found in trees and put the black charcoal onto the sore eyes.

Some of the medicines used in Arnhem Land are very similar to traditional medicines used in Indonesia. Scientists think that the Yolngu traded with Indonesians for at least 400 years. Indonesia is quite close to northern Australia, and the Indonesians are good sailors, fishers and traders. The Indonesian sailors and the Aborigines probably traded their medicines with each other.

However, a lot of the precious knowledge that

the Aborigines built up over tens of thousands of years has been lost, so there are not many details about the medicine they practised. They did not keep written records and, as Aborigines were pushed out of their traditional areas and the tribes were broken up, it became very difficult to pass specialised knowledge down to the younger generations.

But as far as medicine goes today, compared with other groups in Australia, Aborigines get a much lower quality of medical care. The easiest way to measure this is by how many of the easily treatable diseases they get.

Just One Drug from Herbs

Every time a person has an operation and they need a general anaesthetic, their muscles have to be relaxed first. One drug that does this job is based on curare. Curare was first used by the Indians of South America. They rubbed a certain leaf onto the tips of their spears when hunting. Curare is very powerful; the hunters didn't have to actually kill the animal with their spear. All they had to do was graze their prey in some way with their spear to break the skin. Enough curare would get into the animal's bloodstream to make it fall to the ground, paralysed. Nowadays, this drug is being used tens of thousands of times each day, all over the world.

Rheumatic fever is a good example. It often starts with a simple throat infection, caused by one special bacteria. The immune system reacts against this special bacteria and, to fight it, pumps chemicals into your bloodstream. (There are many different types of bacteria, and so the immune system has to make many different chemicals.) By a terrible coincidence, one of the chemicals that attacks this particular bacteria also attacks your bone joints and your heart. Luckily, it's very easy to treat rheumatic fever with antibiotics, but Aboriginal people often don't have access to antibiotics when they need them. On average, Aborigines are 40 times more likely to get rheumatic fever than non-Aborigines. In fact, Aborigines in the Northern Territory have the highest rate of rheumatic fever in the entire world — 614 cases out of every 100,000 people!

The average length of life for Aborigines is very low — the average non-Aboriginal male will die at the age of 73.5 years, but an Aboriginal man in the Northern Territory will die at an average age of just 47 years.

At the same time the death rate for babies is very high. The Infant Mortality Rate measures the number of babies that die in their first year of life out of every 1000 babies that are born alive (not all babies are born alive — some are born dead). The non-Aboriginal population of Australia has one of the best Infant Mortality Rates in the world — on average, only 5.7 babies die out of every 1000 babies that are born alive. This figure of 5.7 is very good by world standards. In the war zones of the various countries that used to be Yugoslavia, the Infant Mortality Rate is about 19 in 1000. The Infant Mortality Rate is 18 in Western Australia and the Northern Territory — even though there is no war going on!

In Australia, as far as medicine is concerned, the Aborigines have lost out twice. Most of them don't get access to our modern medical system, and they don't have their old traditional medical ways.

One Australian medicine developed since white settlement is an oil made from eucalyptus leaves, first produced back in 1854. A Victorian pharmacist, Joseph Bosisto, started to make it when he was investigating oils taken from local eucalyptus trees at Dandenong Creek, near Melbourne. He went into business and sold eucalyptus oil as Bosisto's Parrot Brand Eucalyptus Oil. It's still sold today. (In fact, around 1910, eucalyptus oils were used to separate metals using the flotation process. You can read about this in the story 'Floating Metals' in *Ears, Gears & Gadgets.)*

In 1933, Sister Elizabeth Kenny began her work in treating people who'd been crippled by polio. She moved and massaged her patients' arms and legs, which was completely opposite to the conventional treatment of the time (keeping the arms and legs still). Clinics using her methods were set up in New South Wales and Queensland, but the medical profession didn't agree with her treatment of patients and she was condemned by a Royal Commission that was set up to investigate her.

However, her methods were welcomed in America. In 1946, a movie called *Sister Kenny* was made, starring Rosalind Russell. The Sister Kenny treatment definitely didn't cure polio, but it made the victims of polio stronger and better able to move around.

Polio affects the nerves, which tell the muscles what to do. In some cases, it can weaken muscles in the chest, so that the patient finds it difficult to breathe.

In 1937, during a polio epidemic in South Australia, Edward and Donald Both built an improved version of the 'Iron Lung'. The Iron Lung had been invented in

An x-ray showing the expensive but effective Iron Lung.

Medical Guarantee

Some 1800 years before the birth of Christ, Hammurabi was the King of Babylon. He came up with the Code of Hammurabi, which deals with many matters, including medicine. You can see part of his Code inscribed on a stone pillar that is kept in the Louvre Museum in France.

The Code has severe penalties for doctors if they make a mistake. It says: *If the doctor, in opening an abscess, shall kill the patient, his hands shall be cut off.* However, the penalty was not so harsh if the dead patient had been a slave — in that case, the doctor just had to supply another slave.

America in 1927, and would expand the chests of polio patients, letting them breath. But the Iron Lung was expensive, and so heavy that floors often had to be reinforced to take its weight! Edward and Donald built a Wooden Lung — from plywood and an electric air pump. It was much lighter and cheaper than an Iron Lung — and worked just as well.

In 1928, Sir Alexander Fleming from Scotland discovered penicillin when he noticed that a mould growing on a glass plate would kill some bacteria. When the war came in 1939, the big goal was to start making penicillin in large quantities. In 1939, Howard Florey from Australia and Ernst Chain from Germany worked with Fleming's original mould at

Oxford University in England to get a strain that would make more penicillin. At this time, there were constant bombing raids all over England. The scientists were terrified that their laboratory would be destroyed and all of their work lost. So, every night before they went home, they would put some of their special fungus in their pockets so that they could always start up the next day at another laboratory if they had to. They successfully worked out how to make penicillin in enormous quantities. In 1944, Australia became the first country to make penicillin for civilians (not just the military) at the Commonwealth Serum Laboratory in Melbourne.

In 1956, the Commonwealth Serum Laboratory developed an antidote for the poison of the redback spider. Saul Weiner spent two years trying to make this antidote. His work involved milking the poison out of thousands of redback spiders, and then injecting it into horses. The horses do not get killed or hurt by the poison, but they still make chemicals to fight it. These chemicals are removed from the horses' blood, and then used as an antidote. This antidote for redback spider poison now saves around 250 lives every year.

But people are not the only ones who get sick. Medicines for animals have also been developed. In 1978, CSIRO scientists perfected a slow-release drug for animals. It's difficult to get an animal to take tablets three or four times a day. It's much easier to give it one tablet every week or so. So the CSIRO scientists came up with a capsule that would slowly release the drug, at an even rate, into the animal over a long period of time.

In 1990, the 3M Company released Difflam cough lozenges. Before this, cough chemicals were always packaged as a liquid, which was messy to carry around. Sometimes, the way you package a drug can be as important as the drug itself. Colleen Wood, a Canadian Australian, worked out how to put an anti-cough drug into a hard sugar lolly. There were two main problems that she had to overcome. First, the temperature of boiling the sugar would normally destroy the active chemicals needed to soothe the cough, and second, it was very difficult to get the same amount of drug in each cough lolly. But Colleen Wood solved both of these problems.

In 1994, the F.H. Faulding Company released a drug called Kapanol, as a tablet that people could swallow. Kapanol, a version of a pain-killing drug called morphine, is released slowly at an even rate over 12 hours. This was a great improvement on the previous ways of giving morphine, which involved injecting it every four hours. Kapanol meant that patients suffering from permanent and severe pain, such as cancer patients, could be treated at home rather than in hospital.

In February 1996, three Australian scientists (Graeme Laver, Peter Colman and Mark von Itzstein) won the $300,000 Australia Prize for coming up with a drug to fight influenza. The flu virus is really hard to fight with drugs, because every year it changes its appearance. So a drug that works one winter generally won't work the next winter. But in 1982, Laver and Colman found one part of the flu virus that always stayed the same. This was a weakness that they could use, if they could find the right drug. In 1986, von Itzstein began looking for the drug that would lock onto this constant part of the flu virus. By 1989 they were already testing it, and in 1993, the American Food and Drug Administration allowed them to test this drug on humans.

By 2002, we had worked out most of the human DNA. Over the next 50 years, this knowledge will lead to a huge revolution in medicine.

In fact, I believe that while I will be in the last generation to die, the young people who read this book will be the first generation to live forever (or at least for 500 to 5000 years, with a healthy 18- to 25-year-old body).

History of Medicine

One of the most famous Egyptian healers was Imhotep, who lived around 2800 BC — nearly 5000 years ago. Not only was he a great physician, he was also the architect who designed the famous Pyramid at Saqqarah.

Some of the oldest known medical writings are Egyptian — the *Ebers Papyrus* and the *Smith Papyrus*. They were probably written around 1600 BC. The *Ebers Papyrus* has a strong medical slant. It has special spells to treat certain diseases, and even tells you the best words to say to the gods to get favourable treatment. But it also includes treatments and drugs that are still used today. Even back then, they knew that castor oil would help get the bowels moving!

The *Smith Papyrus* is more surgical — it tells you where to apply pressure to stop bleeding, and even deals with various parts of the body such as the eye and the heart. In some ways, the *Smith Papyrus* is similar to modern surgical books — it tells you about the history of a disease and how it normally progresses in a human being; it tells you what symptoms to look for and what treatments to use; and it even tells you the side effects of some of those treatments.

In Greece, the legends say that the knowledge of medicine was given to Asclepius by the god Apollo around 1200 BC. Temples in honour of Apollo were built in Delphi, and words carved into the stone of these temples discuss the treatment of various diseases.

One of the most famous Greek healers was Hippocrates, who was born in 460 BC, on the island of Cos. (Researchers are not really sure if Hippocrates was just one person, or many.) His ideas are summed up in some 70 books that were written either by him or by his followers. He recommended that people should become healers only if they loved other people. In fact, he specifically said that wanting to get fabulously wealthy was not a good reason for becoming a doctor.

Hippocrates said that details of each patient and their disease should be carefully written down. He also advised that a healer should use all the senses (smell, sight, taste, hearing and touch) to work out what disease the patient was suffering from. Hippocrates was correct about many things – he also believed that while some people were born with particular diseases, other diseases came from the outside world and were caused by factors such as the person's job, the climate or their diet.

In India, one of the earliest famous healers was a Hindu physician called Caraka (or Charaka), who practised medicine around 1000 BC One of the greatest medical textbooks in India, the *Ayurveda*, was written around 900 BC.

By 500 AD, Indian medicine was quite sophisticated. One Indian surgeon, Sushruta (or Susruta), had already worked out that mosquitoes carried malaria, and that rats could carry the plague. He personally knew the medical properties of over 700 different plants, and described some 1120 separate diseases. In his writings, he describes how to treat broken bones, how to deliver babies via Caesarean section, and how he personally removed cancers and kidney stones. He wrote about the different types of instruments that the good surgeon should have and said that most of the instruments should be made of steel.

The Indians probably invented plastic surgery. Back then, one common legal punishment for wrongdoing was amputation of the nose. Indian surgeons could repair an amputated nose by transplanting flesh from the cheek or forehead to what was left of the nose. They could even repair cataracts in the eye, by moving the location of the lens inside the eyeball.

One of the earliest Chinese medical textbooks is the *Nei Ching*, or the *Yellow Emperor's Book of Medicine*. The version that we have today was written some time around the third century BC – but there are claims that it dates back to 3000 BC! By that time, the Chinese healer Hua T'o was not only using drugs (anaesthetics) to put patients to sleep for operations, but he could also operate on the gut and even remove a diseased spleen. The Chinese invented acupuncture, and they knew how to immunise themselves against smallpox. Some Chinese drugs that we still use today include iron (for anaemia), kaolin (for diarrhoea) and adrenaline (usually made by your adrenal gland, but also extracted from the herb muhang, *Ephedra vulgans*, which is used to treat asthma and allergic conditions.)

Roman medicine around the time of the birth of Christ was very good in the field of public health. In fact, their systems to deliver clean drinking water and to remove sewage were not equalled anywhere in the Western world until the 1800s.

One famous doctor, Galen, began working in Rome in AD 161. He was one of the first healers to realise that the arteries and veins carried only blood, not blood and air.

Another famous Roman doctor, Aulus Cornelius Celsus, wrote eight books on medicine. Six of these books are mostly medical — they involve drugs, diet, massage and manipulation. But the last two books are surgical — they discuss how to remove a swollen thyroid gland or a stone in the bladder, and how to repair a hernia. The books even discuss how to remove cataracts from the human eye. Soranus of Ephesus was an expert on women's diseases, childbirth and children's diseases. Normally, a baby inside a mother's uterus should be lined up so that the head comes out first. Soranus was the first to describe what to do if the baby was lined up feet-first — just use your hands to turn the baby around.

The Western Roman Empire collapsed in the fifth century AD, and for the next 1000 years Europe fell into the Dark Ages. During that time, the Muslim Empire kept knowledge of medicine alive. This enormous empire stretched from Persia (today called Iran) to Spain.

One famous Muslim doctor was Rhazes. He was born around AD 860, near where Tehran (the capital of Iran) is today. He wrote several medical books, including a very famous one that clearly described the difference between measles and smallpox.

Another Persian was Avicenna, who lived from AD 980 to AD 1037. He has been called the Prince of Physicians. He was very clever, and had memorised the Koran (the Muslim holy book) by the time he was 10 years old. When he was only 18 years old, he was made physician to the Muslim court. His most famous medical book, *The Canon of Medicine*, was still used in France as recently as 1650.

The World's First Prepaid Postage

Australia had the very first prepaid postage. 'Prepaid postage' means that the sender pays for the mail with some type of stamp or identifying mark. This meant that for the first time, once you had written your letter, you could simply drop it into any letterbox. There were no further payments. Before this, mail had been paid for by the person who received it, not the sender.

This was a revolution. Suddenly anybody, not just government officials, could easily send a letter to anybody else. If the person to whom the letter was addressed was not at home, the post officer could just leave the letter in the receiver's letterbox. There was another advantage. Before prepaid postage, if the recipient refused to take delivery of the letter, there was no fee paid and the postal delivery system made a loss. This new idea of having the sender pay for the mail was as big a revolution in communication as the telephone.

A system of sending written information from one place to another has been around for at least 4000 years. But for practically all of that time, this system was available only to government officials, not to the average citizen.

The ancient Egyptians had such a system by 2000 BC. By 1000 BC, the Chinese had a similar system. The mail was carried by riders on horseback, who would leave their tired horse at a relay station and pick up a fresh one. The relay posts were about 9.5 km apart. This kept the mail moving. Confucius, who lived from 551 to 479 BC, penned a saying which indirectly praised the efficiency of the postal service: *The influence of the righteous travels faster than a royal edict by post-station service.* By the time of the Sung Dynasty (960–1270 AD), mail could be sent 200 km per day if it were urgent enough.

The ancient king of Persia (now Iran), Cyrus the Great (who died in 529 BC), started up a fantastic postal service. The road between Sardia and Susa was then about 2575 km long. In 430 BC the Greek historian Herodotus, wrote that there were 111 relay stations on that road — about 23 km apart. Herodotus wrote what has become the unofficial motto of postal services around the world: *Neither snow, nor rain, nor heat, nor gloom of night stays these couriers from the swift completion of their appointed rounds.*

The Roman Empire also had official couriers who carried messages and small packets for government use. Information was written on parchment, papyrus and even wax tablets. A message could travel up to 80 km per day under normal conditions, and 160 km if there were an urgent need. In a real emergency, the mail could travel 270 km in 24 hours. But when the

Postman for 90 Years

For 90 years, the postman for Windsor in New South Wales was Tom Cambridge! There were three of them. The first Tom Cambridge had the job from 1835 to 1862. When he retired, he passed the job on to his son, Tom Cambridge. In turn, Tom Cambridge passed the job on to his son, Tom Cambridge, who kept it until 1925.

Roman Empire collapsed, it took until the 1800s for a post service as fast and reliable as the Roman one to appear in Europe.

In the 1200s the University of Paris set up a special post service to carry money and letters between students and their parents — but this service was available only in France. In 1477, Louis XI set up a Royal Postal Service with relay stations and horseback riders. In 1481, England set up a similar system.

In 1635, Charles I of England made the postal service a royal monopoly. It took a six-day round trip to get a letter and its reply from London to Edinburgh and back. The cost of the mail was based on how many sheets of paper you used and the distance it had to be carried. A single sheet of paper cost 2 pence per 80 miles. The idea of a postage stamp still had not been invented.

Great Britain had been almost constantly involved in wars (either with France or the rebel colonies in North America) from 1775 to 1815. This was very expensive, and some of the money to pay for these wars came from high charges on the postal system — these even continued for 25 years after the wars were over.

Beginning in 1835, Roland Hill of England looked carefully at the postal system and suggested radical improvements in his 1837 pamphlet 'Post Office Reform: Its Importance and Practicability'. He realised that the main cost of running the system came from the administration — the running of the system! The actual cost of shifting the mail from one place to another was only a small part of the total

Longest-Running Stamp

Australia has the world record for the longest continuous use of a single stamp. The 5-pence green stamp of New South Wales was issued in 1855. It remained in use until 1913 – a total of 58 years.

costs. He came up with a new system where the cost of the mail depended only on the weight. The cost should be same regardless of the distance. He suggested a cost of a penny per half ounce. He was also the first person to suggest that the payment should be made in advance by 'labels' that you stuck to each letter with a special 'cement'.

But government prepaid postage first happened in Australia.

James Raymond came to Sydney on 12 April 1826. In May 1829, he was made the Principal Postmaster of New South Wales. Governor Bourke promoted him to the position of Colonial Postmaster-General in December 1833.

Raymond was well aware of the writings of Roland Hill in Great Britain. He liked Hill's ideas, and he introduced prepaid postage on 1 November 1838. Australia was the first country in the world to do this. The Post Office sold folded sheets of note paper which had already been embossed with a seal.

They cost 1½ pence each, or 1 shilling and 3 pence per dozen. The user would write on the note paper, fold it and seal it, and place it in an official letterbox.

Two years later on 1 May 1840, Great Britain introduced its first stamp — the 'Penny Black'. On 8 May, the 'Twopence Blue' was released. The idea of the postage stamp was a great success. Twice as many letters were carried in 1840 as in 1839. But cash flow from the mail plummeted. This was because the charges were based on weight, not distance. In fact, it took until 1875 before the revenue climbed back to the 1839 levels.

So this change to the British postal system actually caused a loss of income — to the Post Office. But the country as a whole gained enormous income,

Size of Stamps

Stamps are usually rectangular, but they have come in all shapes — circular, oval, triangular, diamond, and even banana-shaped. Stamps also come in many sizes.

According to the 1993 *Guinness Book of Records*, the largest stamp ever issued was the Express Delivery of China stamp, released in 1913. It is 24.75 cm by 7 cm.

The smallest stamps were issued from 1863 to 1866 by the Colombian state of Bolivar. They're 0.78 cm by 0.94 cm.

because the average citizen could now communicate with anybody else in Great Britain. This made it much easier to do business and make money.

Brazil (1843), the cantons of Geneva and Zurich in Switzerland (1843) and the United States of America (1847) rapidly set up their own prepaid postage systems. (Actually, a private post officer in New York had started using his own stamps in 1842, but that was just a temporary local business.) As each country began to use stamps, they put the name of their country on them.

But Great Britain and Switzerland don't have their countries' names on their stamps!

When Great Britain began using stamps, it was the only country in the world to have postage stamps. If you saw an envelope with a stamp on it, you knew that it had come from Great Britain. So Britain didn't need to identify its stamps. So even today, while Australian stamps say *Australia* somewhere on the stamp, and New Zealand stamps have the words

Largest Postal System

The largest postal system in the world is the United States Postal Service. Around 1990, there were 780,000 workers in some 40,000 offices across America. The United States Postal Service shifts nearly half of all the mail in the world.

Airmail Went Nowhere

The first official American airmail flight didn't happen – at least, not on the first takeoff. Once he had become airborne, the pilot discovered that the fuel tank had not been filled! He had to land in a cow pasture to refuel.

New Zealand, the stamps of Great Britain have only *Postage* written on them.

The postage stamps of Switzerland don't have the name *Switzerland* on them either. Instead, their stamps say *Helvetia*, which is the ancient Latin name for Switzerland.

To show that the paper stamps had been used, they were marked with black ink. The black mark left on the paper stamp was called a 'postmark'. But the main colour on the Penny Black was black. Sometimes the black postmark would land on the black part of the stamp, and so it wouldn't show up. This meant that a dishonest citizen could then reuse the stamp. So the British Government rapidly introduced the 'Penny Red' to replace the Penny Black. Even so, over 65 million Penny Blacks were printed.

In 1854, Henry Archer perfected a perforating machine to make those little holes that you find in sheets of stamps. This meant that you could just tear

Cheapest Stamp

Hungary issued the cheapest stamp ever in 1946. It had a face value of 3000 pengo — when 604.5 trillion pengo were equal to 1 cent!

the stamps apart — you didn't need scissors to separate them.

Almost as soon as postage stamps were being used in Great Britain, the habit of collecting them began! In 1841, the *London Times* carried an advertisement that read: *A young lady, being desirous of covering her dressing-room with cancelled postage stamps, has been so far encouraged in her wish by private friends as to have succeeded in collecting 16,000.*

The first official name for stamp collecting was 'timbromania', from 'timbre', the French word for stamp. But this word soon fell out of favour. In 1864, the Frenchman Georges Herpin invented the word 'philately'. ('Philos' is Greek for love, while 'ateleia' means 'that which is free of further tax'. Once you have bought a postage stamp and stuck it onto an envelope, you don't have to pay out any more money or tax.)

Stamp collecting is easy to get into. If you ask your neighbours, you can quickly get lots of used stamps. You can also buy them cheaply. Your stamp equipment is reasonably inexpensive — just an album, some special adhesive hinges and maybe some special to hold the stamps with.

Some stamps can be worth lots of money — especially if they are very rare or have a mistake on them. In 1856, British Guiana released an octagonal magenta 1-cent stamp — and only one of these stamps has ever been found! It last sold in 1980 for $935,000. A Penny Black stamp, postmarked 2 May 1840, on a special First Day of Issue Envelope, sold in 1991 for $24 million.

In 1918, the United States Postal Service released a 24-cent airmail stamp showing a picture of the Curtiss JN-4 biplane. This plane was commonly called the 'Jenny'. On just one sheet of 100 stamps the picture of the Jenny was printed upside down. In 1989, a block of four of these 'inverted Jenny' stamps sold for $1.1 million.

Stamps have created wealth in other ways. One thing that stamps encouraged was new forms of transport — the Pony Express in America, the stagecoach, the steamship, canal boats, trains, cars and planes. Each of these new forms of transport was well paid to carry the mail as rapidly as possible — so government postal services actually subsidised each new form of transport in its early days. But possibly the greatest wealth that came from stamps was the fact that they let people communicate with other people anywhere, very cheaply. And Australia played a big part in this revolution.

Index